CROWDED LIVES

CROWDED LIVES

LINDSAY TANNER

PLUTO
PRESS
AUSTRALIA

First published in 2003 by
Pluto Press Australia
7 Leveson Street
North Melbourne, VIC 3051
www.plutoaustralia.com

Copy edited by Michael Wall
Cover designed by Peter Long
Production by Kathryn Lamberton, Bridging the Gap
Typesetting & page design by Hazard Press Ltd
Printed by Griffin Press

Australian Cataloguing-in-Publication Data

Tanner, Lindsay.
Crowded lives.

Includes index.
ISBN 1 86403 272 3.

1. Interpersonal relations - Social aspects. 2.
Interpersonal relations. 3. Political culture. 4.
Community organization. I. Title.

302.5

CONTENTS

For Andrea

ACKNOWLEDGEMENTS

I would like to thank Megan Alsop and Tony Moore from Pluto Press for their commitment to publishing this book, and their assistance in bringing it into being. My thanks also to my staff Peter van Vliet, Mary Day, Barbara Andrews, Alison Grant and Ben Barnett for their assistance, particularly to Barbara for typing the manuscript and putting up with endless revisions.

I also would like to thank the staff of the Parliamentary Library for their help with research tasks, and Michael Wall for editing the manuscript.

Special thanks to Michael Schluter, Andrea Tanner, Sharan Burrow, Tony Douglas, Peter Lewis, Carmen Lawrence, Lou Farinotti, Simon Marginson, Stephen Howells and Kate Lundy for providing insightful critical comments on the manuscript.

Most importantly of all, my deepest thanks go to my wife Andrea, whose support and inspiration lie at the heart of my efforts to develop a new approach to politics and society.

INTRODUCTION

This book is about human relationships. Relationships with partners, friends, parents, children, relatives, colleagues, neighbours, even businesses. It's about the central role relationships play in our society, and how we consistently undervalue the importance of relationships in our decision-making processes. It seeks to develop the argument in a section of my earlier book *Open Australia* in which I first canvassed the importance of relationships in public discourse, and to build on the pioneering work of the Relationships Foundation in Britain.

Our lives are built around our relationships. We define ourselves by our relationships. In many respects we exist for our relationships. Although many people focus on sexual relationships as the number one factor in social behaviour, it is the broader web of all human relationships that governs our lives.

In the world of stress, change and choice most of us now inhabit, our relationships are under great pressure. We're working longer and harder, separating from our partners and children more, living alone more, moving more. Many of us no longer live in a neighbourhood, a small world of strong interconnecting relationships built on trust, informality and respect. Instead we participate in a variety of limited relationships with people we barely know, while the core framework of key relationships – the ones that really matter to us – is eroding. With less time for family and community involvement we're creating a society with less connection, more alienation, and more loneliness. We are leading more crowded lives, but slowly losing our sense of connection with each other.

Relationships are the missing piece of the political puzzle. As we struggle to adapt to the domination of the bottom line and to constant economic, social and technological change, the factor invariably omitted from the equation is human relationships. We've managed to insert the environment into our political calculations, but we still neglect the factor that drives and sustains our existence.

In *Crowded Lives* I make a case for placing relationships at the front of our thinking in politics and public policy. I consider several major public issues from a relational standpoint, particularly the links between work, education and community, parental relationships with children, and our social and biological relationships with each other.

The shape of our future society will be determined by the health and strength of our human relationships. Our economic progress will depend on the relationships that sustain our economic activity. Our society is wealthier than ever before, but we're still struggling to protect our threatened and abused environment and totally neglecting the health of our relationships. We must refashion our entire approach to organising our society, and put relationships at its heart.

1

NEEDING EACH OTHER

We all define ourselves by our relationships with others. Our answer to the question 'who are you?' is very often about who we work with, who our friends are, who our parents are, who our children are, who our brothers and sisters are, who our neighbours are. We answer this way because we largely live for our relationships. Though some people like to define their identity by their possessions or achievements, we're all ultimately defined by our relationships.

Just to exist in our complex modern world we need help from other people. In some form or other, most of us are employed helping others, and we all depend on others for the basics of life. Someone else usually makes our clothes, grows our food, builds our house, makes our car, writes our books and educates our children.

Our modern social democracy has focused overwhelmingly on the *economic* aspects of helping each other – 'who does what?', 'who gets what?' Recognition of the central role of interdependence in our lives has been dominated by talk of the production process, government and laws. Since the Industrial Revolution, the material aspects of human relationships have dominated politics in developed nations – imposition of taxes, distributing the rewards of the production process, and regulating economic behaviour. The economic relationship between the individual and society underpinned the twentieth century's cataclysmic conflict between capitalism and communism, and the ultimate compromise outcome of this conflict, social democracy.

In recent decades other themes have emerged in western politics. Feminism, environmentalism, racial equality, sexual liberation, civil liberties and peace have dominated the concerns of a growing number of people in western societies. Usually promoted by economically advanced and educated constituencies, these themes have cut across traditional conflicts about the creation and distribution of resources.

Some of these issues, such as environmentalism and peace, reflect an extension and abstraction of inherently economic concerns. A high standard of living, for example, is clearly threatened by overexploitation of the environment or participation in major military conflict.

Other themes reflect notions of personal liberation from social oppression. Feminism, gay liberation and racial equality all seek to remove socially imposed structures governing relationships. In each case, demands for individual freedom are gradually prevailing over decaying social frameworks that reflect levels of technology, education and living standards of a bygone era.

Although these economic progress and personal liberation themes still dominate politics in western societies, they are becoming a little stale. The particular debates they now sustain are often just faint echoes of past titanic struggles. And while the outcomes of these struggles continue to shape our politics, a new set of themes is slowly emerging. These themes reflect the long-neglected but ultimately crucial issues to do with *human relationships*. In a world dominated by economic and social individualism, the time is ripe for a new focus on the responsibilities we owe to each other.

While older struggles will continue, more and more our political attention will focus on the nature and content of human relationships. The post-war wave of technological, economic and social change has completely reshaped the structures of human relationships in western society, and the emerging biotechnology revolution promises to alter even more radically the nature of who we are and how we relate to each other.

Virtually all politics reflects the tensions between the interests of society and the interests of the individual. With economic survival issues invariably dominant in political debate, relationship issues have not been prominent. Governments and political parties have largely ignored these issues, perhaps assuming that they are the responsibility of priests and psychologists. This tendency to ignore the centrality of human relationships has sometimes led to government decisions that are actually harmful to relationships. Decisions and transactions that carry economic benefits can also carry relational costs, which are expensive in the longer term and ultimately undermine social sustainability.

It is time for us to examine our society through the lens of human relationships. We need to consider how contemporary issues affect relationships, and develop approaches that strengthen our relationships with each other. To move beyond the individualism of western societies in recent decades we must move beyond the relatively mechanical approaches of traditional social democracy. In spite of Ben Chifley's warning that Labor's mission is about much more than an extra sixpence in a worker's pocket, Labor has tended to focus on the material aspects of human society, and neglected the serious issues that emerge from the nature of our relationships with each other.

By living crowded lives we are slowly eating away at the bonds which connect us with our fellow human beings. If our pursuit of economic progress is not modified by a concern for the health of our relationships, we will start losing those things in life which are most important to us.

The challenge to build a better society now involves issues that have previously been seen as essentially personal. The nature and strength of our connections with others is fundamental to how we live our lives, and it should be fundamental to how we organise our society.

2

ALONE IN THE CROWD

Relationships are central to the wellbeing of individuals and society as a whole. Our relationships with friends, family, colleagues and neighbours govern our sense of identity, self-worth and belonging. Relationships within communities give us social support networks that govern our existence as individuals. In old age we draw on the relationships we've invested in over our lifetime, rather like having a relational pension. The more affluent we are as a society the more important these relationships become in determining our ultimate happiness and wellbeing. Without them we are adrift, lonely, disconnected.[1]

These relationships are heavily affected by our circumstances and surroundings, including the actions and decisions of governments. Government solutions to economic problems will not work if they're not also beneficial from a relational perspective. According to the Relationships Foundation, a British organisation dedicated to promoting better relationships, one of the primary causes of failure in providing housing for homeless people in Britain is that they miss the friends they made on the street.[2] Giving a homeless person a public housing flat is no solution if it isolates them from their social networks. Economic assistance that damages relationships doesn't necessarily improve the lives of the people who receive it.

Relationships Foundation director Michael Schluter is a passionate, caring man with an extraordinary capacity to combine serious policy analysis with a profound understanding of human behaviour and human needs. I was first introduced to Schluter's work by Peter Thomson, an Anglican priest and educator renowned for his role as a mentor of Tony Blair. He gave me a copy of *The R Factor*[3] by Schluter and David Lee, said a single emphatic word to me – 'friendship' – and insisted that I read it.

Our lives, Schluter and Lee argue, are built around our relationships of friendship and family. These relationships govern our actions and our aspirations. They provide the setting in which we live our lives. Relationships are also fundamental to business activity. Trust is essential to the pursuit of economic improvement. The lack of close relationships and trust creates additional costs that hamper economic efficiency. Employees who can't be trusted to do their work diligently have to be closely monitored and supervised. Suppliers who can't be relied upon to provide good-quality products have to be checked. Customers who can't be trusted to pay have to be tied down by formal contractual arrangements and credit assessments.

Just as poor relationships translate into major business costs, good relationships are at the heart of the inherent value of a business. Some relationships are even recorded formally as assets in balance sheets, such as goodwill and distribution networks. Others, like contacts and broader networks, can be critical to the success of a business. These relationships have an intrinsic as well as a functional value. Individually they deliver specific outcomes for a business. Collectively they provide the context in which the business exists.

HOLLOW DECISION-MAKING

Government decisions, social and political institutions, work organisation and community culture are all factors that impact on our relationships. Transport decisions affect our ability to visit friends. Telephone prices influence our capacity to stay in touch with loved ones. Shopping hours laws change the way we spend our weekends. Family laws govern how we relate to our children. Workplace rules dictate how much spare time we have to spend with family and friends. Entertainment options affect the way we form sexual relationships. Insurance rules impact on how our children play in the local park or on a sporting field.

Yet we rarely examine political issues from a relational angle, and hardly ever systematically analyse the impact of our decisions on human relationships. No matter how central such factors may be in people's lives, we remain trapped in a mechanical framework of issue analysis. Governments run relationships programs, like the Howard Government's Family Relationships Services Program, but they're invariably focused on the symptoms of relational problems in our society, not the overall health of the broader web of social relationships. We teach our children practical skills so they can compete in society as adults, but devote little effort to teaching them to develop and maintain good relationships. Complaints about decisions like mass closure of bank branches remain isolated and outside our ideas framework. They're rarely transformed into central elements of public policy. Though it can be hard to measure, the negative impact of such changes can be far more central to people's lives than the gains in efficiency they may bring.

We've built a society in which we have less time for our children, less interaction with our neighbours, less involvement in the community, and less participation in collective activities. Longer working hours, greater dispersion of families, more solitary entertainment options and more formalised links between government and citizen have all contributed to this pattern.

Until now, with public policy dominated by economic concerns, we've lacked a broader ideas framework to give form and substance to these issues. To develop such a framework we could start by combining an examination of the relationships effects of decisions into a systematic relational analysis. By creating a set of ideas around the aim of building better relationships, we can reforge our public policy tools. Concerns about the impact of change on families, friends and community can be dealt with as essential elements in decisions, not external factors.

In *The R Factor* Schluter and Lee develop an analysis of these issues built on observed changes in the patterns of human relationships. Their analysis provides a road-map for understanding relational problems in contemporary society, and a framework of priorities for tackling them.

Relationships between human beings are conditional – they involve giving and receiving. They are rarely equal, with each party providing exactly the same value to the other. Many are built on the notion of differential giving and receiving, either through different kinds of contribution or contributions delivered at different times. Parents bring up children who in turn will care for them in their old age. Other relationships involve more altruistic contributions, where the benefits to the contributor come in the form of pride, happiness or contentment. Some involve passing on a benefit, where a person receives from one person and gives to another. Mentoring relationships, and more formal arrangements like apprenticeships, are usually built on this concept. Some relationships involve contributing to a pool, such as a group of friends, and receiving benefits from that pool. Many relationships are extremely unequal, but continue because of the very limited bargaining power of the less powerful partner. Women who remain in violent and abusive relationships are sometimes in this situation.

CHOICE AND OBLIGATION

According to Schluter and Lee,[4] our relationships are all constructed around a complex web of choice and obligation. Formal and informal social arrangements create all sorts of relationship obligations. Parents are legally required to care for their children. Married couples vow to look after each other 'in sickness and in health'. Social norms oblige people to care for close relatives such as frail elderly parents. Other relationships, such as friendships and casual sexual relationships, are essentially governed by choice. Sex without commitment is a relationship without obligation.

The old saying 'you can choose your friends but you can't choose your relatives' neatly captures this tension between choice and obligation in human relationships. It also provides a clue to the enormous variety in the choice-obligation mix in relationships in different cultures. Forced or arranged marriages are common in cultures where obligation greatly outweighs choice in human relationships. In some cultures, choice, even in friendships, is heavily constrained by race, religion, caste or other factors.

Schluter and Lee believe that the technological revolution and ensuing cultural change in western societies in the latter part of the twentieth century has radically changed the balance between choice and obligation. Choice is now almost totally dominant, and virtually all obligations have become highly conditional.[5]

Rising affluence and advances in transport and communications have created social opportunities rarely seen in earlier times. We are now infinitely more mobile, meaning our social choices are less tied to the obligations of the past. People are more anonymous, and therefore less constrained by the threat of social disapproval. Most of us inhabit a 'mega-community' of large numbers of people whose relationships with each other are transient and conditional.[6] We interact with many more people than our forebears did, but we have fewer deeply committed permanent relationships and therefore a much lighter burden of social obligations. Our new world is like a call centre where workers spend their time relating not to other workers a few feet away but to the voices of people they don't know and will never meet. We are alone in the crowd.

In my study of community life in the Melbourne suburb of Brunswick in the 1920s, I found a community that was virtually an island in the middle of a large city. Cars and telephones were rare, and public transport was rudimentary. When children grew up and married they often moved into houses in the same street as their parents. My study of Sands & McDougall street directories revealed that roughly half of those who moved house between 1924 and 1928 moved to another house in Brunswick. A large proportion of the remainder moved to the adjoining suburb, Coburg. Most people worked near where they lived, and participated in community activities only in Brunswick.[7] Even in the

1950s, the fact that my Brunswick-born mother married a man from south of the Yarra was an object of some comment and curiosity.

Since that time technology has massively widened our horizons, changing the nature and scope of our relationships. Even in more remote rural areas this change is apparent. I recently returned to my old home town of Orbost to speak at the local secondary college. Although most of the students seemed to be children of kids I grew up with, I found that the contemporaries I remember best from my childhood in Orbost are now living in Scotland, Thailand, Singapore and provincial Queensland, with another only recently returned after spending twenty years in Papua New Guinea. Increased personal mobility has transformed the nature of relationships, even in small country towns.

With this much wider scope for connecting with others, our relationships are more conditional, anonymous, and mediated through large institutions. The trust, loyalty and respect that tend to flourish in direct relationships become much harder to establish. With more and more of our relationships moving to a national and even international level, we're losing the local intimacy of neighbourhood and slowly turning from neighbours into numbers.

Many of our relationships are now one-dimensional. My doctor is only a doctor. The police officers in my area are only police officers. I don't know them as friends, husbands, mothers, local footballers or service club members. A shared occupational and educational background now transcends that of location and neighbourhood. In my inner Melbourne electorate, complex social sorting mechanisms ensure that the middle-class professionals don't mix with the low-income public tenants in high-rise flats. Their children even attend different state schools. In some cases there are primary schools within walking distance of each other that have radically different student populations – one for the professionals' children, and the other for kids from the flats. Other schools have partly become commuter schools, where city workers from all over Melbourne bring their children each day. The negative effect this has on their children's ability to sustain friendships outside school hours, because of the great distances separating them from their friends, apparently doesn't concern them.

Our relationships in the mega-community are ruled by formality. We interact with many more people, but pay the additional costs associated with contractual arrangements and formal transactions which were previously conducted directly and informally.

In some cases, it is true, the negative aspects of the mega-community have generated a community response, such as Neighbourhood Watch and community banking. Instinctively people understand there's more to activities like banking and security than anonymous contractual arrangements, and that reviving the relationships these activities were once built on can be very productive. Bendigo Bank's model of community banking is a good example of relational thinking applied to an economic problem. The model is succeeding because it meets the relational needs of small businesses and individuals ignored by the major banks, and because it requires individual communities to mobilise in order to make it work. Bendigo Bank provides the banking infrastructure, but the community has to provide a board of directors and several hundred thousand dollars of initial capital.

Overall, however, the world we now inhabit gives us more opportunities to avoid social obligations than it does to build them. It opens up options which were not really available to our forebears. It fosters individualism, and creates winners and losers. It empowers individuals to secede from their social context, to search for a new context, or even to create one.

Some young people enter sexual relationships on a 'you'll do for now' basis. Some middle-aged people make contact with their elderly parents once or twice a year. The less attractive and less intelligent are readily excluded from peer groups. We now take it for granted that we have the freedom to withdraw from relationships we have grown tired of.

Individualism is so rampant in our society that people are virtually able to construct their own social identities. The ties that bind people to family, friends and place are much weaker than they once were. We have the power to exercise a much wider range of choices, and we usually do so.

Sometimes the decision to change social context is forced on us by economic circumstances. If a company moves from Melbourne to Sydney, workers may be forced to choose between their economic wellbeing and their social relationships. Webs of personal and family relationships can be virtually destroyed by a decision to relocate a factory. The relational cost of such decisions is largely ignored in our industrial relations system.

FREE BUT LONELY

The profound change in the balance between choice and obligation lies beneath all of the major social changes and social problems of recent times. Since the late 1960s, crime, drug abuse, family breakdown, gambling, suicide and antisocial behaviour have increased substantially. More people live alone, and more children grow up in disrupted family circumstances. Parental and teacher authority over children has eroded. Individuals have experienced an enormous increase in personal freedom, but our society has paid a price through a substantial increase in social problems.

Older people are more readily abandoned to a lonely existence by absent families. Retrenched middle-aged workers are cut loose from their primary source of personal identity and recognition, with little hope of regaining it. Individuals carry the appalling label 'loser', the modern social equivalent of 'leper'. All this creates fertile ground for drug abuse, gambling, alcoholism, violence and suicide.

Social exclusion is not restricted to poor people. The most poignant expression of the devastating effects of social exclusion I've seen came in a long letter from a middle-class single mother in Melbourne's eastern suburbs. Her description of the social devaluation she experienced in a middle-class suburban community as a result of leaving her abusive husband and battling to care for her four children on her own, made for harrowing reading. Many of her former friends deserted her, and her church tried to persuade her to return to her husband, effectively suggesting that she was in the wrong. Her sense of isolation and loneliness came through in every sentence of her letter. Our society gave her a degree of choice earlier generations did not enjoy, but not the social support necessary to make the exercise of that choice truly worthwhile.

More and more people feel excluded, alienated and despairing. The proliferation of gambling, drug abuse, suicide and family breakdown reflects this surge in social dislocation. For many Australians, neighbourhood is anonymous, marriage is temporary, hard work is less appreciated and decent behaviour seems to go unrewarded. For some the new world of individualism and choice is a bitter one.

In *The Corrosion of Character*, Richard Sennett provides telling illustrations of personal disorientation in the new world of work. He contrasts the emotional stability of Enrico, an elderly cleaner, with the social turmoil and family tensions of his highly paid consultant son, Rico. He explores the impact of modernisation on workers in a Boston bakery, where demanding heavy work done in groups has been superseded by computers and automated machines. He finds a dramatic change in work relationships, with workers in the new antiseptic environment indifferent, transient, and lacking occupational identity and self-respect.[8]

The free market system depends on an elaborate network of community relationships and social trust in order to function properly. A system based on contractual relations requires a certain level of social predictability and long-term stability. Rampant individualism is undermining the very economic system that champions the interests of the individual. Without an underpinning of social inclusion and economic co-operation, a market system will ultimately descend into gangster capitalism.

Greater economic freedom has been accompanied by greater loneliness, alienation and loss of community. Better transport and communications combined with weaker family and social structures has also generated a great deal of social dislocation. Deregulation of the market has helped erode the web of human relationships on which our society is built. Our crowded lives are built on foundations of isolation and distance.

In a tightly constructed society built on relationships of obligation, loneliness is usually not a major social problem. In a sense, people are obliged to associate with those around them whether they want to or not, and they tend to adapt accordingly. Some are still excluded in such societies, sometimes quite brutally, as relationships built on obligation can breed conformism and intolerance. In 1950s rural Australia, people lacking wealth, education and beauty generally did not find it difficult to find a social context in which to belong. Yet those who did not fit in with community norms, such as unmarried mothers and gays, were often ostracised.

The pendulum has since swung dramatically in favour of choice, and a different pattern of social exclusion has emerged. When relationships are dominated by choice, some miss out. Like people at an old-time school dance, the attractive pair off and the unattractive are left on the sidelines. In an individualistic world, people are valued for their wealth, appearance or education, and their innate humanity is barely relevant. A social market is emerging, parallel with the traditional economic market.

Human beings are driven by a survival instinct and a need to receive recognition. We build self-esteem from the approval of our fellow human beings, and we can achieve this only in a communal context. Every individual's worth is measured by other individuals in comparison with other individuals. Our survival as a species has been based on this mechanism of integrating individuals into the group. Mutual recognition is the glue that holds human society together, and enables us to act collectively as well as individually.

In a world of relationships built on obligation, virtually everyone is guaranteed a certain level of recognition. Automatic membership of a group such as a family or tribe carries with it a degree of recognition which transcends personal characteristics. In a world of atomised individuals choosing who to associate with, there is little automatic recognition. It has to be gained by the individual. Those who start with limited advantages face an uphill battle.

The social market for recognition has, like the economic market, been deregulated. By letting our responsibilities towards each other become optional, we've allowed all the inequities of the market to permeate our social existence. The 'recognition rich' get richer, and the 'recognition poor' get poorer. People who are less attractive, less educated, less wealthy and less confident experience greater social pressure and greater social exclusion. The raw impact of economic disadvantage is therefore magnified substantially.

Robert Reich has described the emergence of the 'sorting mechanism' in modern societies in his recent book *The Future of Success*.[9] Economically comfortable people can exercise choice and escape from poor neighbourhoods, poor schools and poor people, and this exacerbates economic inequality. A similar sorting mechanism is also at work in human relationships. Pursuing rational self-interest much less constrained by social obligation, we abandon unloved relatives, shun unattractive peers, and ignore less fortunate citizens. Economic costs to society flow directly from human isolation, particularly additional health costs. A recent study published in the *Medical Journal of Australia* found that loneliness and isolation are major contributing factors to coronary heart disease.[10]

Hugh Mackay has dubbed today's young people the 'options generation', whose first question is always 'what else is there?'[11] Although he argues that young people are developing new informal mechanisms of social inclusion, there can be little doubt that his assessment captures the ethos of the new world of relationships dominated by choice. Personal freedom and individual choice tend to dominate most political debates. The fact that greater freedom for some may disadvantage others is barely noticed.

The widespread feeling that we are losing control over our own lives is directly linked with the new supremacy of choice in human relationships. Greater freedom means greater insecurity and instability. A wider range of variables means less control. New and increased risks must be confronted, like the risk of your spouse leaving, your child rejecting your authority, your friend moving overseas, or your neighbourhood being threatened by crime, drugs and vandalism.

RECONNECTING PEOPLE WITH POLITICS

Relational analysis developed by the Relationships Foundation provides a starting point for a new way of looking at these issues. It doesn't seek to bring back the old constraints or formal obligations that have faded. It looks to strengthening relationships by placing relational issues at the centre of decisions about all the issues that govern the way we live our lives. It seeks to maximise individuals' ability to form and sustain strong relationships, and to reduce the threat to these relationships posed by individualism and social exclusion. It seeks to promote strong family relationships, healthy personal relationships and fulfilling friendships. It seeks to counter atomisation and to rebuild community. 'Relationism' seeks social sustainability in the same way that environmentalism pursues environmental sustainability. Like our natural environment, our 'social ecology' is in great need of repair.

Often I encounter situations where undervaluing the importance of relationships lies at the heart of a serious problem. Recently I gave advice to a friend who was seeking nine months' leave without pay from her job so she could deal with some major family problems. Even though she's a valued and skilled employee with a very good track record, her large public sector employer wouldn't let her take this leave. By ignoring the central importance of her close relationships they were creating a lose-lose situation. Either they lose a valued and experienced staff member and she loses her job, or she lets her family problems fester and her employer ends up with a distracted, disgruntled employee.

This story emphasises how, even in economic transactions, relationships are critical. Governments seeing citizens as 'customers' may produce economic benefits, but at what relational cost? Because it's hard to measure the impact of positive relationships, governments and corporations often overlook important relational issues when making decisions. Western societies are awash with social problems like excessive working hours, loneliness, job insecurity and stress, but any attempt to tackle these problems tends to crumble when confronted with the tyranny of the economic bottom line. The recent debate about gambling is a good example of the growing tension between economic and social imperatives.

The lack of an analytical framework that lets us factor relationships into our decision-making is a critical weakness in governance today. We've made some progress in balancing economic objectives with environmental considerations, but we generally ignore the relationships dimension. Loneliness and insecurity may be obvious consequences of particular decisions, but they're rarely even taken into account in the decision-making process. Like environmental damage once was, they are seen as mere 'collateral damage'.

Schluter and Lee suggest that a relational philosophy can be built on five basic concepts:

- all human life has intrinsic value and dignity
- good relationships are central to personal and social wellbeing
- good relationships are built on a broad balance between choice and obligation in the social structure
- good relationships must have a sound moral underpinning
- economic and social policy should be aimed at sustaining relationships, not undermining them.[12]

The Relationships Foundation has developed practical techniques to measure and analyse the state of relationships inside organisations and the impact of decisions on relationships. These include 'relational audits' and relational policies for areas such as health and criminal justice. In a relational audit a detailed assessment is made of a company's inner workings, and how its internal structures and processes impact on relationships between the people in the organisation, and between them and the people they seek to serve.[13] Such an audit often reveals, for example, that workers and managers getting together informally on a regular basis can greatly improve the inner health of the organisation, which ultimately improves its bottom line results.

The Foundation looks at relationships from five distinct angles:

- underlying commonality of purpose
- parity of power and authority

- number of connections
- continuity and stability
- directness of communication.[14]

A relationship built on shared goals, relatively equal partners, multiple points of connection, continuity and direct communication is likely to flourish. A relationship in which these factors are largely absent is bound to fail.

The outcomes of relational analysis can be very practical. The Foundation discovered that British housing authorities take no account of the proximity of close family members when allocating housing for single parents.[15] As the support of the extended family is critical for most single parents, this approach makes no sense. But it is entirely predictable in a society that makes decisions with only economics in mind.

Similar Australian examples can be found of misguided government decisions which damage relationships. The Howard Government's attempt to impose voluntary student unionism on Australian campuses is a prime example of the pursuit of economic individualism at the expense of human relationships.

When I arrived at Melbourne University as a 17-year-old from the country, I knew virtually no-one, and I'd been on campus only once before. It was the student union that helped me integrate into the university community, participate in collective activity, develop friendships and build a sense of identity and belonging. Through running and funding countless clubs, activities and structures, student unions set the scene for individuals to form new relationships. They give people somewhere to belong.

The Government's commitment to destroying student unions is simply a recipe for less association, less chance to participate and, ultimately, more social exclusion and loneliness. It promotes individual economic freedom at the expense of better relationships.

Mackay suggests that the one word that best sums up the contemporary yearnings of the Australian community is 'village'.[16] In other words, our society is reacting against the anonymity, formality and impersonal remoteness of the mega-community. People worry that they no longer live in a neighbourhood.

Our task is to strengthen relationships and thereby rebuild neighbourhoods. Relationships and neighbourhoods come in different forms, but they are what ultimately make communities healthy and vibrant. We can't directly create or control relationships and the neighbourhoods that sustain them, but we can change our ways of making and implementing decisions so that we protect and nurture them.

Major political decisions should be informed by an analysis of their likely impact on human relationships. A proposal should be assessed against relational benchmarks as well as economic and environmental benchmarks. Does the location and design of a housing estate make it easier or harder for parents to spend time with their children? Does a local decision-making process bring neighbours together or separate them into competing groups? Is a community facility run with direct community involvement, or top-down direction by remote bureaucrats? Does the government assist community-based credit and security initiatives? Does the administration of justice focus on rebuilding broken relationships?

It's common for Cabinet decision-making to include standard reference points such as financial and environmental impacts. Past attempts to introduce relationship considerations have struggled for credibility because they've been driven by a desire by conservatives to bring back traditional family values and attack the reform agenda of social progressives.[17] The partisan politics implicit in the *family* impact statement could be replaced by a politically neutral *relationships* impact statement. We should be able to bring relationship issues into our decision-making processes without reigniting the culture wars between progressives and conservatives.

Since the introduction of accrual accounting in the Federal Budget, a framework of outcomes assessment has been built into the Budget process.[18] Though still new, this framework gives us the chance to build relationships impact assessment into the core of our decision-making. It invites us to consider the notion of outcomes literally, and examine the broader impact of government decisions beyond the narrow bottom line.

The concept of triple bottom line accounting – economic, environmental, social – offers some prospect of bringing relationships into corporate decision-making. To date the social component has been mostly to do with particular relationships, such as with a company's employees. Corporate philanthropy and issue management are other factors often addressed in the social section of the triple bottom line framework.[19] The concept of relationships impact may provide a coherent, unifying theme that is currently missing from this part of triple bottom line accounting.

Placing relationships at the heart of our political and economic discourse will radically change the way we approach major issues. While continuing to pursue greater economic efficiency and better economic outcomes, we'll make our decisions in the much broader context of our human relationships. By making better relationships and greater social participation a stated policy objective we'll be able to put community at the centre of our political debate. In contemporary Australian politics, much of the debate is sterile and mechanical, focusing only on money matters. What can we expect from this but community alienation from politics? A much broader political discourse, incorporating the true realities of people's lives such as their human relationships, will help reconnect people with politics.

3

BEYOND LIBERATION

The fundamental changes in human relationships that are reshaping our society reflect the wave of social change that has occurred since the 1960s. Since that period, community attitudes on most social issues have changed enormously. Sixties revolution themes of individual freedom, feminism, environmentalism, racial equality, sexual and gay liberation, and opposition to war and nuclear weapons have completely changed western society. Initially absorbed mainly by the radical fringe, these attitudes have since permeated much of mainstream society. Although there's still plenty of resistance to the progressive social agenda of the sixties, and in some instances it struggles to get majority community support, these themes are still the most potent influences shaping our society's approach to a broad range of social issues.

DO YOUR OWN THING
The sixties revolution was produced by powerful forces of individualism and libertarianism, which grew out of structural economic changes during the post-war boom. Rising affluence and technological change meant that for the new generation basic survival was guaranteed, and issues of choice, leisure and personal fulfilment took priority. An explosion of tertiary education, white collar professional employment

and consumer choice helped to generate social change throughout the western world. Although often clothed in trendy chic left-wing garments, at its essence this revolution represented a profound triumph for individualism and atomisation. The real driving force behind the revolution – despite expressions of solidarity for the Viet Cong, China and Cuba – was an ethos of personal liberation, sexual freedom and self-fulfilment. The slogan 'do your own thing' is a much more accurate reflection of the sixties revolution than 'power to the people'. Driven by technologies as diverse as television, electronic musical equipment and the pill, an ethos of creativity, freedom and personal gratification took hold of our society, leaving no institutions unchanged.[1]

The outcomes of these changes have been immensely liberating. The role of women in society has changed fundamentally. Freedom of sexual expression is widely accepted, and homosexuality is no longer a criminal offence. The stifling cloud of censorship has lifted, and our television has been transformed. Racism no longer has the explicit legitimacy it once enjoyed. Prison-like institutions that once housed mental patients and wayward children have been closed or radically reformed. Authority, and in particular the deployment of police or military force by those in authority, is much more widely questioned. Environmental issues are now more central in public debate.

Yet there has been a downside to this story, one largely ignored by the proponents of these changes. Our community has paid a significant price for its liberation. The removal of many restraints on various forms of social behaviour has seen a huge increase in social problems. Crime, gambling, family breakdown, drug abuse, suicide and teenage delinquency have soared since the sixties. Many deinstitutionalised mental patients have been left to fend for themselves, liberated from virtual imprisonment but denied the assistance necessary to find a new social context. As social structures have broken down, more people have succumbed to social exclusion, loneliness and alienation.

The role of parents in raising children has changed substantially. In earlier generations most children grew up with mothers and fathers with narrow and clearly defined gender roles. Now some children have fathers who perform the primary carer role while others have fathers who are totally absent. It is hardly surprising therefore that the nature of parental authority over children has changed. It is equally unsurprising that many who were brought up in the old environment feel that the moral fabric of the community is unravelling.

The individualism of the sixties has been absorbed and magnified by the materialism and consumerism that also grew out of the post-war boom. Personal gratification has become a primary driver of economic activity. Consumer debt has ballooned and saving has declined as more and more people live for today and let tomorrow look after itself. In some instances, these powerful forces in the consumer economy also drive the behaviour underpinning many of our most serious social problems. In a society that promotes instant gratification, excitement and risk-taking as legitimate consumer choices, is it any wonder that we have major drug abuse and gambling problems? When children are bombarded with advertising promoting thrills, risks and excitement, is it surprising that many turn to recreational drugs? The most damning word in the lexicon of the modern child is 'boring'. If excitement is the primary goal of human existence, drug abuse is inevitable, no matter what sanctions we employ against it. The dramatic increase in gambling – rooms full of solitary punters throwing their money down the slot – also reflects this pattern. The widespread social problems associated with excessive gambling are the price we pay for our obsession with excitement. As with drug abuse, chronic gambling becomes a substitute for healthy relationships.

Since the sixties our society has gradually reorganised itself along much more individualistic lines, with major negative social cons-equences. Philosophical frameworks that gave a collectivist perspective on life, such as traditional religion and socialism, have seen their influence ebb away. Participation in organised community structures like service clubs, churches and trade unions is dropping as well. In a world where choice has prevailed over obligation, people tend to make selfish choices. The fact that the aggregated impact of millions of individual choices produces negative consequences for some people rarely troubles those making the choices, because the connection between individual choice and social outcome is so remote.

For those of us who've absorbed and grown up with sixties liberation ideals, the idea that our core beliefs may have negative consequences is hard to face up to. The left has little to say about the social problems of recent decades. Having lost the debate around the supposedly overwhelmingly economic origins of these problems, people on the left now virtually ignore them. How many prominent figures on the socially progressive side of the political spectrum tackle big problems like crime and family breakdown?

While a desire for liberation and personal freedom was a totally appropriate response to the stultifying, oppressive and discriminatory environment of that era, we've failed to notice that the world has since moved on. Simplistic concepts of liberation no longer provide the answers to contemporary social problems. Our most pressing problems are a reflection of insufficient social order and security, not an absence of personal rights and freedoms. The liberationist left has little to say on the very serious issues of social disintegration facing western societies. Those still proclaiming the sixties social movements as the foundations of a revived left are like old generals fighting the last war. Those of us who fought and largely won the great liberation battles of the sixties and seventies must confront the negative social consequences that also flowed from the great social upheavals of that era. These social problems have not been caused by the rise of feminism and sexual liberation, they are parallel consequences of technological change and growing affluence. The sixties revolution is not the cause of the enormous social problems of our time, but its proponents still have a responsibility to tackle these problems. So far we've failed to take that responsibility seriously, allowing conservatives like John Howard to monopolise genuine community concern about these issues, and to twist that concern to suit their political agenda.

TUNE IN, TURN ON AND ... PARTICIPATE

As Hugh Mackay points out, every society has a 'guiding story'.[2] Until the sixties, basic materialism was the driving force in western society. The themes of liberation and personal development which then overtook materialism have all but exhausted themselves. We need to build a new guiding story for our society. Rebuilding the health and strength of our human relationships is an excellent place to start.

More individualism offers no solutions to our most pressing community problems, but nor would any strategy to reverse the improvements in individual freedom that have flowed since the sixties. Trying to turn back the clock would be both ineffective and wrong. Nostalgia for a world we have outgrown will not provide solutions to the problems of the new world.

We need to build a new intellectual framework that moves beyond narrow concepts of rights and freedoms and seeks to integrate the interests of the individual with those of the society. Since the effective collapse of state socialism, social democratic parties around the world have been adrift in a philosophical vacuum, trying to swim with an individualistic tide while clinging desperately to fading collectivist origins. Developing a new response to the problems of social decay is part of the broader challenge of building a new guiding story for social democratic politics.

What should our society offer to each of its individual members? Many of the great contemporary philosophers have grappled with this question. To John Rawls it's an ability to pursue one's own life plan.[3] To Ronald Dworkin it's equal concern and respect.[4] To Amartya Sen it's a capability to achieve.[5] I see such approaches as a little too individualistic, in that they downplay the significance of the web of broader social relationships we are part of. A more appropriate concept, which focuses on the relationship between individual and society and between each individual and other individuals, is that of a capacity to participate in society.

If individuals develop recognition only through their relationships with other individuals, the opportunity to have a viable social context starts to resemble a fundamental human right. If we are social animals, we therefore have a need, indeed a right, for somewhere to belong. Our society has an obligation to all its members to ensure that they can participate in society.

A quick glance at some social issues will show how important we think this principle is, without perhaps even realising it. We instinctively understand that young children should be raised in an environment of love and nurturing, and that mere satisfaction of material needs is not enough. Our response to the horrors of the Stolen Generation is eloquent testimony to our innate understanding that belonging is a fundamental human need. We correctly dismiss the claim that stolen Aboriginal children were much better off in material terms as irrelevant.

Broken or fractured relationships are a central element in social and economic dislocation. Many people lose connection with their wider family, often through no fault of their own. The loss of emotional mooring provided by parents, grandparents, siblings, uncles and aunts can have a very powerful impact on an individual's life. Some refugees face the challenge of building a new life without even knowing if close family members are alive or dead. This loss of belonging is very difficult to overcome.

A capacity to participate implies an opportunity to form and sustain viable and worthwhile relationships, both economic and social. It suggests our society has an obligation to ensure that all its members can genuinely belong. This principle is at the heart of recent efforts to eradicate discrimination against people with disabilities. It underpins the traditional Labor commitment to access to quality health services, education and training, employment opportunities and personal security. It reflects our understanding of telecommunications services as essential services that enable people to stay in touch with loved ones.

A capacity to participate is about opportunity, but much more than equality of opportunity, which is a narrow concept entailing winners and losers. Instead the ability of individuals to participate meaningfully in society through strong and healthy relationships must be at the centre of our considerations. The impact of specific policies on human relationships should be as important as their impact on the Budget bottom line.

All politics is about subjugating the power of the market. Those who are threatened by the untrammelled power of market forces invariably turn to politics as the solution, sometimes in extreme forms like fascism and communism. Many of the great twentieth-century battles between markets and politics have been fought to a standstill. Rising affluence has dimmed the intensity of conflicts over the distribution of wealth. Yet the negative effects of markets on social participation have not been properly addressed. Issues of human relationships and recognition have often been part of important battles over the distribution of wealth, but they've rarely been prominent in their own right.

Broader concerns about the quality of human relationships and the capacity of individuals to participate in our society are slowly moving towards the top of the political agenda. It's time to refocus, and elevate these concerns even further in our priorities. The days of crude materialism are over. In the new era, politics will be more about relationships, recognition and human dignity. Although money matters will still be central to politics, broader relationship concerns will no longer be as peripheral as they have generally been over the past century. The role of social capital and the strength of relationships within a community are now recognised as fundamental factors in the economic and social wellbeing of that community. Although material wellbeing has improved dramatically in recent decades, overall levels of happiness have not. Without better relationships, more money does not necessarily mean more happiness. Money won't always solve the relationship problems in crowded lives. Expensive presents for our children are no substitute for love and attention.

Much of our social existence is built around an array of community organisations and institutions. Community health centres, service clubs, neighbourhood houses, libraries, sporting clubs, residents associations and play groups are just some of the organisations present in all Australian communities. Some are government bodies, some are funded by government, and some are quite independent of government. Their role is widely underestimated because of our failure to recognise the central importance of relationships in human existence. With the left traditionally preoccupied with the role of the state, and the right championing the rights of the individual, the contribution of this intermediate sector has often been overlooked.

The important role of such organisations is now recognised even by economics researchers. University of Massachusetts academics Samuel Bowles and Herbert Gintis conclude in a recent study that in order to understand an economy it is necessary to analyse local communities and associations, as well as markets and governments.[6]

A word often found in the objectives of service clubs points to the real role many of these organisations play. That word is fellowship. These clubs aim to create a social context in which individuals can build friendships, participate in activities with like-minded people, and develop a place to belong. In some cases participation in these activities arises from narrow economic motives, such as building contacts and networks to sustain a business or profession. More often, however, they reflect the power of the basic human urge to associate and belong.

On any given Saturday around Australia you'll find countless rather ordinary sportspeople participating in a wide array of sporting contests at levels where fellowship and belonging are as important as competing and winning. Others find roles in coaching, umpiring, scoring and just generally helping out. This social context gives their lives an additional dimension, and a framework around which many relationships are built. When my brother moved to a small country town outside Melbourne recently, the first thing he did was to join the local cricket team. The common ground of sporting participation provided him with an easy path to integration into the local community.

Playgroups provide similar benefits for young parents. Neighbour-hood houses offer an environment of care and friendship for a wide range of people, particularly those who suffer some kind of social dislocation. The Home and Community Care program alleviates loneliness and isolation among older people. Saturday morning sausage sizzles bring together many people who are committed to helping others through their church or charity. Tenants' associations on large public housing estates provide a framework for community activity and interaction.

In the wake of mounting individualism, these community organisations are under threat, their numbers shrinking. The public liability insurance crisis is adding to the burdens of voluntary community organisations. Longer working hours and increasing entertainment options are crowding out opportunities for social participation. Intensification of work is crowding out opportunities for people to participate in community activities.

Governments should intensify their commitment to sustaining community organisations like these. Our capacity to participate in society depends on access to economic wellbeing, access to services, and access to community life. If we're to tackle the mounting problems of loneliness, exclusion and isolation in our society, sustaining the bonds of community and relationships must become an important objective of public policy.

A good society must be built on hope. Strong healthy relationships nurture and sustain hope. Isolation and loneliness destroy it. If we can improve the social frameworks around which we all build our relationships, we'll generate countless tiny grains of new hope in relationships throughout our society. The beneficial consequences of more hope, more confidence, and more commitment will be enormous. Our economic wellbeing, security and relational health will all benefit.

4
PERSONAL RESPONSIBILITY

The vital component in human relationships that seems to be under siege from all sides in the modern world is the notion of personal responsibility. With choice prevailing over obligation in society, the rules governing our behaviour are becoming something of a one-way street. Political discourse is dominated by concerns about individual rights, but there's not much focus on personal responsibility.

Greed, selfishness and bad behaviour seem almost to have become entrenched as the new community standards. Courtesy, modesty and self-restraint are very definitely out of fashion. The triumph of individualism has created a world where self-sacrifice seems quaint and self-restraint irrelevant.

The outcome of this change in patterns of behaviour has been a long-term undermining of community confidence in institutions, a reduction in levels of social trust, and an increase in general cynicism. The social contract governing the way we relate to our major institutions seems to be slowly unravelling.

To the average citizen, it seems that powerful people and organisations routinely get away with breaking the rules. Big companies are able to wriggle out of obligations to their workers and customers. Smart lawyers and accountants promote tax avoidance schemes and help criminals evade justice. Children defy parental and teacher authority. The rich and powerful use their muscle to exhaust weaker opponents in unequal legal battles, and escape serious punishment for offences like drink-driving.

The rules and institutions that used to govern our behaviour seem to have fallen apart. For the ordinary citizen it often feels like people can get away with anything if they're rich enough, smart enough, or brazen enough. The way we now deal with each other seems to involve no respect and no trust.

As a worker you're now on your own. The notion that your boss has to comply with a set of rules designed to protect you is out the window. If your employer goes broke there's a serious risk that you will lose the entitlements owing to you.

As a customer, you're treated with disdain. Giant companies treat you as a number, hit you with higher prices on every front, and offer ever more complicated products designed to milk a few extra dollars out of you. If you have a problem, you end up spending hours or even days trying to get redress.

PLEASE PRESS 1...

Dealing with large organisations can be a nightmare. You start by wrestling with automated phone systems that present you with options that never quite fit your problem. Once you've eventually managed to make contact with a human being you find that they're in a call centre at the other end of the country and have never heard of the place you live in. If you're lucky, you get some action, but it usually involves someone else in the organisation who's never heard of the person you first spoke to. When the whole thing breaks down you can spend ages tracking down the original person because they've refused to give you their direct line or full name. The whole system seems designed to make you give up in disgust and go away. Many people do. The well-connected and the powerful have informal mechanisms for dealing with such problems, while most ordinary citizens are left on hold.

The widespread reorganisation of major companies and government bodies which has created this parody of customer service has been driven by the need for efficiencies and cost reductions. The cost of these changes has been borne by our relationships with each other.

The automation of customer service has been characterised by a decline in trust, a loss of job satisfaction and an increase in hidden inefficiencies caused by preventing workers from using their own common sense. The web of human relationships which sustains our society has deteriorated as a result. Much of the difficulty in dealing with problems has been pushed back onto the individual customer.

Older Australians who lament the passing of the intimate world of personalised service and practical assistance are not unduly nostalgic or irrational. They're unhappy about the loss of the small degree of human comfort provided by established relationships with those who satisfy their everyday needs and wants. The angst, stress and inconvenience of living in the newly automated world hardly seems worth benefits like fractionally cheaper phone calls. Human relationships may not appear in the company accounts or the household budget, but they still matter a lot in our daily lives. For many people, having a little more money to spend is poor compensation for having to live more crowded lives.

The desire for fair and proper rules and decent treatment lies inside many major political controversies. Workers' entitlements, corporate collapses, tax avoidance, lenient sentencing, consumer ripoffs and poor school discipline are all issues that reflect this profound community need. People are tired of being mistreated as consumers, tired of being mistreated as workers, and tired of seeing others exploit loopholes in the rules or evade punishment for breaking them.

LEGITIMATE FEARS

Community concerns about rising crime and ineffective sentencing are often dismissed by civil libertarians as ignorant and misguided. As well as being inherently patronising, this attitude essentially misses the point. Although there can be no doubt that sensationalist media dramatically overstate the prevalence and magnitude of crime in our society, fears about community safety should be accorded respect and legitimacy, not dismissed as irrational.

We all carry irrational fears, where threats are exaggerated or imagined. Behavioural science studies have demonstrated how little connection exists between human fears and statistical levels of actual risk.[1] No matter how much data there is proving that driving a car is more dangerous, many people will always be more frightened of flying.

Fear of crime may be misplaced or exaggerated, but it affects people's lives and relationships. If an elderly woman is too frightened to leave her home it's hardly sufficient to tell her that her fears are grossly exaggerated. Developing more genuine awareness of the real risks of crime is important, but this should be based on the starting assumption that fear of crime is both genuine and legitimate. It's not acceptable for our society to allow some of its citizens to live their lives imprisoned by fear. Acting more vigorously to address the causes of their fear, whether through prevention, detection or punishment, is absolutely essential.

In some of the high-rise housing estates in my electorate, tenants live in a state of perpetual fear because drug users and dealers have virtually taken over the public spaces in the buildings. Laundries, stairwells and landings are littered with needles, and the tenants live with the mess, the noise, and the fear. Occasional police clamp-downs have some effect, but then the problem just shifts to another inner-city estate. Because our society can't deal with drug use and antisocial behaviour, many low-income tenants are frightened to go outside the front doors of their own flats. They end up virtual prisoners in their own homes.

Appropriate punishment for criminal behaviour is essential so that people can live good lives and enjoy their relationships with others. Community concern about lenient sentencing reflects deeper feelings about the decline in personal responsibility in our society. It shouldn't be dismissed as mere tabloid hysteria.

Punishing criminal behaviour has a number of objectives that are central to our criminal justice system: deterrence, rehabilitation and protection of society from further crimes spring to mind. But we often forget the importance of punishment. The desire to punish wrongdoing is a very powerful human emotion that almost invariably dominates the feelings of victims of crime and their immediate families. For those struggling to come to terms with the loss of their murdered son or the emotional damage of their raped daughter, a feeling that justice has been properly applied to the perpetrator is a very important part of the process of recovery. The absence of that feeling can have a crippling effect on the ability of a crime victim, or their family, to resume normal life.

By appropriating to itself a monopoly on legal violence – in the form of imprisonment and other punishments – the state stands in the shoes of victims of crime, and undertakes to take retribution on offenders on their behalf. This role is fundamental to any civilised society, and without it society would degenerate into a self-perpetuating cycle of violence.

The debate about lenient sentencing is about much more than complex arguments about deterrence, rehabilitation and costs of imprisonment. It's ultimately about the state fulfilling its responsibility to impose appropriate punishments so that victims and their families can move on, and that the risk of people taking the law into their own hands is kept at bay.

It sometimes seems that this point is lost sight of in the process of sentencing people who've committed serious crimes. Although the law shouldn't become a vehicle for personal vengeance, it must stand the test as an alternative to personal vengeance. The recent upsurge in community anger about 'soft' sentences may not be entirely coherent but it mustn't be ignored. If there's a widespread community view that sentences for particular serious crimes are inadequate, the state has to respond. If the issue isn't dealt with in a considered way, more crime victims will take the law into their own hands, and sentencing will become more erratic and arbitrary. Governments will ultimately go too far and bring in crude mandatory sentencing initiatives that produce perverse outcomes and further undermine the integrity of the criminal justice system.

RELATIONAL RESPONSES TO CRIME

While the 'lock them up and throw away the key' approach is popular with some, dealing with this issue requires a great deal more than merely increasing prison sentences. The concept of restorative justice, in which perpetrators are required to apologise and give some kind of compensation to their victims, may offer a new sentencing option that strengthens the legitimacy of community punishment without simply adding to prison terms. Although it may not be appropriate in some cases, the notion that offenders have to pay a debt to their victims as well as to society at large could allow us to reinforce the punitive element of the criminal justice system in a more socially constructive and less expensive way. A sense of moral payback – with the offender making a public apology or other acknowledgement of the need to repay a debt to society and individual victims – would strengthen the credibility and effectiveness of sentencing and parole systems, and make it easier for victims of crime to get on with their lives. What it's really doing is making the offender take personal responsibility for their crime.

The concepts of 'relational justice' pioneered by the Relationships Foundation offer several options for reform.[2] Relational justice relies on notions of shame and apology, and reflects elements of approaches taken in some traditional cultures, where forcing offenders to confront the consequences of their acts, apologise personally to victims and accept public shaming by their peers is a major component of the system of justice. These strategies are being pursued in New South Wales through justice conferencing, where young offenders are required to meet with their victims. Rates of re-offending have fallen significantly for those offenders involved.[3]

Such strategies will only work in some cases. Shaming can be a very powerful factor within a relational framework based on respect, such as is often found in indigenous communities. Further stigmatising an offender without any genuine relational context is likely to be counter-productive. Short-sighted efforts like making a 12-year-old shoplifter wear a T-shirt saying 'I'm a thief' only make matters worse.

Building stronger community relationships is also essential to tackling crime and fear of crime. Crime thrives on anonymity, isolation and reluctance to 'get involved'. The stronger neighbourhood relationships are, the greater the inherent resistance to criminal behaviour. Most violent crime involves people who know each other. The restraining bonds of community can perform an important preventive and deterrent role in the battle against violent crime.

Personal security is a central element in the way we all relate to each other. For a society to function properly, its members must enjoy a high level of personal security, and the institutions and laws that maintain security must be built on widely accepted notions of fairness. Communal retribution for wrongdoing is a legitimate part of this framework. For people to feel secure and accept that the state is fulfilling its responsibilities, justice must be seen to be done.

The progressive approach to crime issues can be quite inconsistent. In some cases, like gun control, industrial manslaughter and domestic violence, stricter laws and more police powers are seen as good things. In other areas they are portrayed as early steps on the road to a police state. We should seek to develop a more consistent approach to law and order issues, based on the presumption that the ordinary citizen is entitled to basic security and protection from crime.

We need to rebuild the framework of rules in our society to reflect the world we now live in. We need to enhance the powers of our umpires, like the Industrial Relations Commission, the Australian Competition and Consumer Commission, the Australian Securities and Investments Commission and the courts. We have a responsibility to ensure that criminal wrongdoing is adequately punished. Our society should be built around clear, strong rules that are properly enforced. This enforcement should be complemented by education and prevention strategies that anticipate and inhibit antisocial behaviour. Community-based strategies like Neighbourhood Watch have a particularly useful role to play.

Our community is crying out for new role models, for people who exert a positive influence on our behaviour. The slow deterioration of our framework of relationships in part reflects years of popular infatuation with dubious role models. In recent times it seems as if mercenary, outrageous and callous behaviour has become the collective benchmark for our society. Since the 'greed is good' 1980s, there's been a noticeable retreat of civility, modesty and self-restraint in Australian life.

Good role models cannot be created. A free media cannot be forced to provide coverage of positive stories. We all have a collective responsibility to promote the role models of decency, fairness, diligence and commitment who still exist in all walks of life. Building a better society based on stronger, more positive relationships requires fair rules and strong umpires, but it also needs behavioural ambassadors, both corporate and individual. In a world where choice has triumphed over obligation in human relationships, people must be persuaded to behave decently. Example is still a very powerful influence on social behaviour.

Personal responsibility is the missing ingredient in many contemporary relationships. Although we can't simply impose such obligations on individual relationships, our society can reinforce its framework of rules and enforcement to elevate the role of personal responsibility in our relationships. 'Doing the right thing' may be unfashionable in some sections of the community, but it's an essential component of a decent society.

5

WORK AND RELATIONSHIPS

The most obvious area of public policy where relationship issues predominate is the widening battleground of work and family. The ability of ordinary workers to integrate the needs and demands of family relationships with their work obligations is emerging as one of the central issues of twenty-first-century politics.

The demand for family-friendly workplaces is slowly crystallising into a clear and coherent program. Unfortunately the potential economic costs of reform are easy to quantify, but the benefits are not. No matter how compelling the stories of individual families may be, they can't be multiplied by millions to produce a national figure representing the total benefit to our society. Although more flexible working arrangements also carry substantial economic benefits for many employers, the raw business cost of family-friendly reforms is a major barrier to change. Bodies fighting for change, like the ACTU, are therefore pushing uphill to achieve changes that will improve people's lives.

Throughout the work of contemporary commentators we hear a common refrain: the economy's strong, individuals are better off, but there's 'something wrong'. That something is the growing stress and pressure on relationships that comes with being part of a strong economy. Our lives are more crowded, and our relationships are buckling under the extra strain.

Many Australians feel they have less time for their spouses, less time for their children, and less time for their relatives, friends and neighbours. When they do have time to nourish these relationships, they're often tired and distracted. They're unable to contribute to, and gain value from, their relationships at anything like an appropriate level. These experiences are often compared with memories of earlier days – which are embroidered by time – meaning the underlying sense of disquiet and dissatisfaction is magnified by a sense of loss.

This 'embroidery' makes comparing relationships today with those of the past difficult, as any measure you use is bound to be subjective. Yet a great deal of politics involves dealing with the subjective experiences of people. The recent surge in community disquiet about relationships, stress and time pressures may be based on an exaggerated sense of loss, but it can hardly be dismissed as a figment of the collective imagination.

However difficult these things may be to measure, many people instinctively feel that something *is* wrong. Mounting social problems like family breakdown, drug abuse and gambling addiction suggest that our relationships are under greater stress than they once were.

If our decisions are informed only by numbers on a balance sheet, these vital issues will simply be ignored. By balancing economic bottom line considerations with some relational analysis, we can readily demonstrate the need for more family-friendly work arrangements.

THE ERA OF SERVICES

Over barely two decades, the Australian economy has changed almost beyond recognition. A world once dominated by factories, farms and mines has been economically transformed by explosive growth in tourism, hospitality, information and personal services. Since the early 1980s employment growth in traditional industries has stagnated, while jobs in childcare, restaurants, creative arts, media, information, tourism and financial services have grown rapidly.[1] As the limits on our ability to consume physical products have retarded growth in traditional goods industries, the new industries in information, hospitality and human services have taken over as the engine of economic growth.

This change has had a staggering impact on the nature of human involvement in the production process. Processes built around physical activity and large machines are easier to organise and easier to measure. They are more susceptible to collective participation and regulated limits on workloads. In the industrial age the production process was built around permanency, security and male dominance of formal work. But now, in the era of services, such dynamics have been turned on their heads. Male muscles are less important, and female mental and relational skills can no longer be left to languish. In the new world of work, permanency and security have given way to speed and flexibility.

The new jobs involve skills that are fluid, always evolving and adapting, usually under-recognised, and often not directly related to formal education. In this new economy work is less structured, more personal and less secure. The skills involved in solving problems, co-ordinating different activities, serving customers, responding quickly to client needs and managing effective communications almost have to be absorbed through experience rather than learned.

In the new world of work, most mothers are in the workforce. Most jobs are less secure. Career paths are less predictable. The boundaries around the individual worker's duties and time obligations are fuzzier. The economic pressures on individual companies are more immediate and more acute.

Just as the dynamics of industrialisation gradually permeated the agricultural sector, the dynamics of the service economy are flowing through into the traditional industrial sector. The economic needs of the newly dominant service-related production processes are beginning to determine how our society is organised, and to dictate the shape of the interaction between work and family life.

The outcomes are clear: workers under more stress, working longer hours in less secure jobs. Around 30 percent of Australian workers are now employed in casual jobs.[2] According to recent ABS data, over 20 percent of workers do unpaid overtime and 60 percent work at night or on weekends.[3] Small business owners face similar challenges. The negative reaction to the GST and deregulated trading hours among small businesses is largely a response to the intrusion of longer working hours and more stress into family relationships.

WORK HARDER, WORK FASTER

These changes in the production process have helped generate the phenomenon of 'affluence fatigue'. Overall incomes are at record levels, three times what they were fifty years ago.[4] Over that time the size of the average family home has almost doubled while the size of the average family has fallen significantly.[5] We spend ever-increasing amounts on non-essential goods and services, many of which are designed to diminish the negative effects of these changes on our working lives. To purchase these things we have to work harder and longer.

The prevailing feature of so many modern consumer goods is saving time. Our microwaves let us reduce food preparation time. Our mobile phones save us the hassle of getting to a landline. Our video recorders let us skip the inconvenience of watching TV shows at difficult times. Our email relieves us of the need to waste time buying stamps and envelopes and posting letters. We buy fast food and pre-prepared meals to eliminate time spent on cooking. We even end up trying to replicate some of the positive aspects of the old production process, like joining a gym to achieve the health benefits of the physical labour most of us no longer have to perform.

We're on a treadmill that's always imperceptibly gaining speed. To buy all these things that save time we have to work more. We've created a vicious circle of time consumption, where the cost is borne by our relationships. We spend less time with our families and friends in order to earn the money which will enable us to buy things like microwave ovens, which will eliminate the need to do certain things together. So we have less time available, and less reason to spend that time doing things together.

Intensification of work is the untold story of our recent economic success. Although the pursuit of greater efficiency and more competition has been central to that success, it has carried a significant cost. We may be producing and consuming more, but we are also crowding the parts of our lives which matter most to us, our relationships with others. Many Australians are crying out for greater balance in their lives as a result.

Clive Hamilton of the Australia Institute argues that we have a problem of middle class over-consumption. The opinion poll data he cites suggests that the new world of work is driving us into ever-increasing work hours, stress and consumption. Although 83 percent of Australians think we're too materialistic and obsessed with money, 56 percent say that they spend virtually all their money on the basic necessities of life.[6] With 30 percent of Australian workers now working more than 48 hours per week, Ross Gittins' rhetorical question is very apt: 'why are we running around as though we've all got only six months to live?'[7] A recent Newspoll survey commissioned by the Australia Institute indicated that almost a quarter of people in the 30 to 59 age-group are responding to this question, voluntarily reducing the extent of their work commitments to enjoy life more, including reducing their status and income.[8] Significantly this survey found this 'downshifting' is occurring as much among blue collar workers as among professionals, and lower-income earners as well as higher-income earners. Thirty-five percent of survey respondents nominated more time with family as the reason for downshifting, with healthier lifestyle, more balance and more fulfilment also figuring prominently. Those motivated by a desire to attain a more environmentally friendly and lower consumption lifestyle represented a relatively small minority of the downshifters. Although the survey was not constructed in these terms, it's reasonable to read 'better relationships' as a broad description of most of the major reasons for downshifting.

As well as doing longer hours, many Australian workers are working harder and faster. In service jobs there are fewer physical limits to an individual worker's input. As competitive pressures on employers intensify, individual workers are loaded up with work obligations which stretch them to the limit. In many occupations, particularly in higher-paid professional employment, the ability to bear ridiculous workloads has become a badge of honour. If we examine these arrangements from a relational perspective it should be a mark of shame.

Research into these problems is still relatively recent and limited in nature. Some argue that greater levels of work stress are associated mostly with higher-income positions, and that more stress is a by-product of conscious choices by individuals.[9] It's more likely that stress has increased across the board. Few workers have the luxury of choosing their exact working hours, incomes and stress levels.

Changing patterns of work are an important contributor to family breakdown, substance abuse and delinquent behaviour. They also contribute to mounting insecurity and uncertainty in personal relationships. Without a clear picture of future employment circumstances, it's much more difficult to commit to a stable relationship, having children, and building a permanent home.

The growing casualisation of the Australian workforce reflects a number of factors, all ultimately connected to changes in the production process. Some are unavoidable, like the explosion in the number of tertiary students seeking part-time work. Others, like the decay in labour market regulation and the increased ability of companies to squeeze their workers, are much less acceptable and should be reversed.

PROTECTING OUR RELATIONSHIPS

Whether through longer working hours, more stress at work or the insecurity of casual employment, changes in the production process are imposing a heavy burden on our human relationships. We can't return to the old world, or seek to reimpose the old world's regulatory arrangements on the new economy, but we can build a new regulatory framework that's explicitly designed to protect our relationships.

The ACTU's battle for two years' parental leave, including eight weeks' simultaneous leave, the right to return to work part time, more flexible rostering and more emergency leave is just a beginning.[10] This campaign should be gradually extended into a broader crusade to protect our relationships from the undue incursion of the new world of work.

Dealing with the issues of work and family is not merely about ensuring that our work doesn't take over our lives. It's about enabling people to manage their relationships better. It's about addressing the double job problem experienced by many working women, and it's also about enabling many men to regain some balance in their lives. According to a 1999 Federal Department of Family and Community Services survey, 68 percent of fathers feel they have too little involvement in their children's lives, and the vast majority of these say the demands of work prevent them from being the fathers they want to be. In addressing the negative impact of work on family relationships, it's not enough to make it easier for mothers to combine work and family responsibilities. We must also enable fathers to assume greater responsibility for maintaining and nurturing their family relationships. Greater flexibility at work should not become a means of perpetuating the inadequate level of male contribution at home.

Almost a hundred years ago in the Harvester Judgment, the presumed economic impact of a worker's relationships was built into our wage-fixing system by Justice Higgins.[11] As the assumptions underpinning this decision slowly crumbled, the regulatory framework changed. We now have a system of labour market regulation which, with few exceptions, presumes that a worker has *no* significant relationships outside work. The enormous growth in variety of human relationships over recent decades has become an excuse for our labour market regulators to ignore relationships altogether.

To ease the pressure on our relationships with spouses, children, family and friends we need to take action to limit excessive work hours and casual employment. What we do will have to be carefully calculated and specific. It should include reinvigorating penalty rates for overtime, making sure employment contracts prohibit blatantly excessive working hours, and extending leave entitlements to cover such things as occasional attendance at a child's school activity. It should also encompass the notion of choice, providing individual workers with the ability to trade one leave entitlement for another. A recently struck agreement between the Federal Department of Education, Science and Training and its staff allows them to reduce salary payments and gain more annual leave, take six months' maternity leave at half pay, and gain childcare subsidies for school holidays.[12]

At present the availability of such choice in the workplace happens only in a very limited way, for example when workers use individual days of accumulated annual leave to care for a sick child. The current arrangements for various kinds of leave tend to be rigid and non-transferrable. In some cases, such as sick leave, there is merit in this rigidity. In others, such as long-service leave, it's difficult to understand. As most workers don't qualify for long-service leave it would make sense to allow them to use this theoretical entitlement for more useful purposes, such as sustaining their family relationships.

Traditional notions of industrial justice have been built on very concrete matters such as wages and occupational health and safety. Despite the explicit demands of the original champions of the eight-hour day, campaigns for shorter working hours have often produced the outcome of higher wages rather than shorter hours. The time has come to place relationships at the forefront of the industrial agenda, as a primary objective of social progress.

While many Australian workers are working longer, harder and faster, and buying more and more things, their human relationships are steadily decaying. No matter how well off we are, our society is poorer when we're unable to sustain strong, nourishing relationships with our families and friends.

6

CONNECTING WITH YOUNG MEN

Our society has a growing problem with young men. All around us we can see the evidence of increasing alienation, anger and violence among younger males.

Over the past decade, school retention rates for boys, already well behind those of girls, have fallen even further behind.[1] Recent Australian Council of Educational Research analysis indicates that boys' literacy levels are inferior to girls', and the gap's widening.[2] Deaths from illegal drugs overwhelmingly involve young men.[3] The incidence of serious assaults, most of which are committed by younger men, increased by 50 percent between 1995 and 2001.[4] Since 1979 the number of suicides of men between the ages of 25 and 39 has increased a good deal more rapidly than for women in the same age group.[5]

Phenomena like road rage point to a latent anger in many young men which can be flicked into violent action by quite trivial events – a toot of the car horn leading to aggressive tailgating or even a knife attack. Many young men are angry and disengaged from society. The only political messages that attract them are negative themes that allow them to vent their anger.

Such men feel alienated from a society which seems to seriously under-value them. In their eyes, many of their attributes are either no longer valued or are even actively repudiated by our society. Social behaviour that was normal twenty years ago is now unacceptable.

This underlying crisis of masculinity can be seen in debates about guns, smoking, road safety, pornography and woodchipping. In each case, our society is effectively telling large numbers of predominantly blue collar men that there's something wrong with them. The cumulative resentment which such social change has generated has become a significant force in our society, to a point where some politicians now seek to exploit it. Victorian Liberal Leader Robert Doyle's recent promise to relax the strict application of speeding fines was a transparent attempt to capture the strength of these sentiments for political purposes.

LOSING STATUS

These trends are external symptoms of very deep changes in our society. Just as technological change is dramatically changing the production process and reducing the importance of physical labour, so the male role in our society is being restructured.

Work has always comprised physical, mental and relational skills. Throughout human history, while a more intellectually oriented minority has always been required for mental work, most men have been physical workers and brawn has been more prominent than brain. Men have hunted savage animals, bashed bits of metal, built skyscrapers, dammed rivers. And through playing this primarily physical role in the production process, men have gained automatic respect, recognition and identity. Within a generation, technological change has virtually inverted this ratio. In the new world of work, raw physical input is on the way down, and intellectual and relational skills are on the up.

Recent research by Mark Cully of the National Institute of Labour Studies at Flinders University on the 1.9 million new jobs added to the Australian workforce between 1986 and 2001 graphically demonstrates this trend.[6] Roughly 1 million of these new jobs are in occupations dominated by mental skills, particularly professional and para-professional jobs. Around 700,000 are in lower-skilled service jobs, such as shop assistants and hospitality workers. There's been virtually no growth at all in jobs requiring substantial post-school training outside the university system. Total employment in skilled trades jobs has actually fallen by 13,000. In other words, employment in traditional male manual jobs is shrinking rapidly as a proportion of our total economy. The growth in professional and personal services jobs offers little consolation to many of those who would previously have slotted comfortably into such manual jobs.

In her landmark book *Stiffed*, Susan Faludi links this loss of dominance in the production process to the decline in the male role of protector.[7] As women have become more independent, men's identity and self-esteem have gradually fallen away.

Young men have seen their fathers accorded a certain degree of respect and recognition because they're manual workers and protectors. Yet as the young men enter the world of adulthood they see they won't gain this respect themselves. Loss of status is a guaranteed recipe for anger and resentment. A subconscious feeling that they are no longer important is eating away at many younger males.

The most common response to these concerns is to blame feminism. This view is totally misconceived. The rise of feminism since the 1960s is a component of these broader social changes, not their cause. Once the raw physical contribution, where men have an advantage over women, ceased to dominate the production process, discrimination between the sexes became totally unsustainable. The battle to eliminate entrenched injustice and discrimination against women must continue unabated. Whatever problems have arisen for men from the waves of change in recent decades, preserving the mechanisms of discrimination is not the solution. To do so would both be fundamentally wrong and have little impact on the underlying causes of male alienation. Restricting opportunities for women would not increase opportunities for those men who are missing out in the new world of work.

Yet we can't ignore the negative aspects of the enormous social upheaval we're living through. If more young men are killing themselves, committing violent crimes and abandoning school, we have to find out why and tackle the problem seriously. Throughout history, great social upheavals have been caused by alienated young men. The more extreme examples of this phenomenon can be seen in the recent growth of violent religious fundamentalism in many parts of the world. Although our society seems under no threat of such serious upheavals, the combustible potential of large numbers of disconnected young men can't be ignored.

THE EDUCATION OF BOYS

The primary focus for dealing with these problems inevitably lies within our education system. It's there that the problems of male alienation tend first to appear, and it's there where much of the solution lies.

A recent report by the House of Representatives Standing Committee on Education and Training paints a stark picture of the growing problems of young males in our education system.[8] Year 12 retention rates for girls are now 11 percent higher than those for boys. The vast bulk of suspensions, expulsions and disciplinary problems involve boys. There's clear evidence that, as a group, boys are much less interested in and satisfied by schools than girls are. In spite of the fact that leaving school early is a recipe for a future of low income and poor prospects, many boys can't wait to leave. A similar pattern has emerged in Britain in recent years.[9]

Evidence from various sources considered by the committee suggests that boys and girls learn differently. Boys respond better to visual learning, while girls are better at verbal learning. Boys tend to respond to structured challenges and direction, while girls flourish through collaborative and self-directed learning approaches.

It seems that the balance between competition and collaboration and between teacher-directed learning and self-directed learning have an impact on educational outcomes for boys and girls. The growing dominance of women in teaching, particularly in primary schools, is also under scrutiny. Three of my seven years at Orbost Primary School were taught by male teachers. Few primary school children now experience this level of exposure to male teachers. Almost 80 percent of primary teachers are female. This lack of contact with male role models and male approaches to discipline, particularly as it is also absent from many homes, may have some effect on young boys.

However, the committee report makes it clear that these issues are a good deal more complex than they seem.[10] Males are still well represented in secondary teaching ranks at 45 percent, and many primary schools are getting fathers involved in classroom activities. Over the past three years I've helped out in my daughter's class three or four times a year, helping with reading and group activities, and numerous other parents both male and female do likewise. I'm doing the same for my son, who started school this year.

The committee found that boys themselves regard teacher gender as being of little significance to their concerns about schooling, and that the increase in single parent families is not to blame for the problems with boys' education. It would also be simplistic and inaccurate to conclude that in recent years girls have been favoured in our educational system, and boys are now suffering. As the committee observes, 'many longstanding patterns of employment disadvantage for women and educational underachievement for girls persist, particularly for girls from lower socio-economic backgrounds'. It also points out that the gap between the performance of boys and girls is greater in lower socio-economic sections of the community.[11]

What then is causing problems for boys at school? The committee suggests that recent changes in the production process are directly implicated in the relative decline in the educational performance of boys. With fewer traditional manual jobs available, and many boys unable to respond adequately to the demands of the new economy, the overall relevance of school for them is declining. Also at fault, they found, is the decline of the extended family and neighbourhood.[12] Once again, the deterioration in broader community relationships is a factor in significant social problems. Crowded lives mean less time and energy to invest in the future of new generations.

But rather than approaching these issues as a tug of war between the interests of boys and girls, the needs of both genders should be pursued in the broader context of these structural economic changes. The evidence considered by the committee suggests that the response to these changes for girls has been more effective than it has for boys. The fact that changes in the way girls are taught have not eliminated entrenched female disadvantage is not a reason for ignoring the changing needs of boys in education.

Our society has a core responsibility to ensure that all its citizens, male and female, have a productive and useful role to play in the community. We have to ensure that everyone has the capacity to participate in our society. Ensuring that everyone has the opportunity to gain appropriate skills and education is central to this obligation. Our ability to build and sustain relationships in a broader community is absolutely dependent on the contribution we make to the community. That contribution is heavily influenced by our education and training systems. Adapting the role of young men to the changing needs of our society requires changing their expectations, recognising the importance of their contribution and connecting them with appropriate opportunities.

The extraordinary paradox in the present position of boys in the education and training systems is that Australia faces major skill shortages in areas like metal, mechanical and electrical trades, traditionally male-dominated skilled manual occupations.[13] The average age of skilled tradespeople in sectors like aviation and telecommunications is lengthening as the training commitment of major corporations falls victim to the tyranny of the bottom line.[14] While the proportion of manual jobs in the economy is shrinking, our society's commitment to skills training for many of those jobs seems to be falling even more quickly.

The recent expansion in apprenticeships and traineeships under the Howard Government has been largely a smoke and mirrors exercise. The expansion has been driven by short courses in service occupations at the expense of the traditional trades areas. Some employers abuse the system in order to get cheap labour. The quality of training provided is highly variable, and, according to the Dusseldorp Skills Forum, the average intensity of training per individual student has fallen. In recent years up to 50 percent of apprentices and trainees have failed to complete their courses.[15]

The expansion of vocational training into areas like hospitality and retail, which began under the Hawke Government in the late 1980s, is both welcome and necessary. Under the Howard Government it's become a smokescreen to hide a declining government commitment to technical training, deteriorating training quality, and employer abuse of the system.

The education problems of boys are also linked to the merging of high schools and technical schools over a decade ago. Although intended to assist the less academically oriented who were previously streamed into technical schools, this reform may have actually disadvantaged them.

As the percentage of students going on to university has soared, less academic students have been largely pushed aside in the collective pursuit of higher university entrance scores. Schools are competing for students, with university admission performance the universal benchmark of secondary education. Instead of opening up greater opportunities for students who would have previously attended technical schools, the merger of technical schools and high schools has seen their interests relegated to a lower status, and programs like Vocational Education and Training in Schools are unlikely to dramatically change the situation. It's no wonder that increasing numbers of boys are leaving school early. From their point of view, the longer they're in school, the less relevant to their interests and needs school becomes.

A NEW ROLE FOR OUR YOUTH

Understanding these issues requires developing a broader perspective, one built around our knowledge of young men and their relationships. The way they relate to their peers, to their families, and to their teachers will provide critical insights into the shape of our education and training needs. Contemporary policy seems to downplay the significance of these relationships and the different educational needs that arise from differences of gender and academic orientation.

This challenge has to be met at the same time as we seek to further reorient education and training to reflect the workplace and production process of the future. We can't turn back the clock by demerging schools or re-establishing the pre-eminence of traditional trades. Those traditional trades are themselves changing rapidly, and acquiring more academic characteristics in the wake of changing technologies.

We've allowed our society to become too focused on academic achievement and too wedded to a narrow education and training agenda. Labor's Knowledge Nation policy for the 2001 federal election in some respects reflected this narrowness. For those who are themselves university educated, it's only natural to focus on the needs of universities when higher education is growing rapidly and suffering enormous pressures and stresses. Unfortunately those remaining, who are still in the majority, tend to get left out.

To increase our nation's skills capacity, to match our labour force with the needs of a modern economy, and to re-engage many alienated young people with the community, Australia must substantially increase its commitment to vocational education and training, develop clearer lines of government responsibility, mobilise more private sector funding, and eradicate employer abuses and poor-quality training programs. This new approach should involve greater Commonwealth responsibility for vocational education and training, better mechanisms of student assistance for Technical and Further Education students, and encouragement for secondary schools to specialise in particular disciplines. Private companies should be required to contribute more to the training of the skilled workers whose future contribution will improve their competitiveness and profits, for example by entering into direct agreements with institutions that train those workers. As well as attracting higher status, trades education should reflect the requirements of the new world of work, such as 'soft' skills like communication, relationship management and self-managed working arrangements. A new approach to vocational education and training also requires better broadband access for education and training institutions and a more rapid transition to e-learning and the new opportunities it offers.

Our government must ensure that everyone has the opportunity to develop skills which will enable them to find employment, build the web of relationships which provide them with sustenance and fulfilment, and participate fully in our society. We should offer all Australians a 'skills guarantee', including a commitment that everyone who completes Year 12 will have access to a place in university, TAFE or apprenticeship-based employment.[16] Our overall goal must be to ensure that all our citizens continue to learn and develop skills, both in the education and training system and in employment. Every worker should be more skilled and employable when they leave a job than when they commenced it.

Australia is falling behind in its education and training effort. Large numbers of Australians may become economically irrelevant unless we substantially increase our commitment to education and training. In particular, a disproportionate number of young men are falling by the wayside because the education system does not adequately cater for their needs.

The relationships we all develop as we grow into adulthood pro-foundly influence our future as adults. These relationships in turn are largely shaped by our relationship with the world of education and training. Our participation in that world can build identity and self-esteem, and generate opportunities and supporting networks. Or it can generate alienation, anger, social isolation and aimlessness. Although the needs of our economy and production process must inevitably dominate our approach to education and training, we must not neglect its broader role in developing strong, well-balanced young people capable of building and sustaining a wide range of positive relationships. Social engagement – just as much as skills development – is crucial to the future health of our economy and society.

7

RELATIONAL PARENTING

One of the crucial areas of public policy most in need of relational analysis is our approach to parenting. In particular, the role of fathers needs to be reconsidered. Although fathers now contribute more to the parenting process than they once did, as the strict boundaries of gender roles have broken down, on average they don't contribute enough.[1] Although it's vital that work arrangements are made more family friendly, such reforms should not simply allow men to continue to avoid their parenting responsibilities. The excessive pressure on working women must be relieved at both ends, in the workplace and at home.

QUANTITY TIME
Until well into the twentieth century, many men played a significant role in raising and mentoring their male children through the world of work. Most boys went to work in their early teenage years, often in the same workplace as their fathers. Others were initiated into the world of work under the watchful eye of uncles or close family friends. Most adolescent boys grew up with male role models who had the ability to exercise genuine authority over them, and who commanded some respect because of their greater expertise and experience in their work environment. Changes in the production process and education have virtually eliminated this connection between fathers and sons, and it

has not been replaced by other equivalent points of connection. Many men have therefore grown up with remote, inaccessible fathers. For many families this means that an excessive burden falls on the mother, and children do not benefit as much as they could from greater involvement with their father.

Although this view is now widely accepted in the community, it has not yet translated into a major change in male behaviour. Concepts like 'quality time' have emerged almost as a way of sidestepping the issue. Although we all want time spent with our children to be high quality, quantity matters just as much. According to a recent Department of Family and Community Services study, the average time fathers spend with their children was the same in 1998 as it was in 1983.[2]

Close personal relationships between parents and children can't be boxed in by concepts such as quality time. Some of the most precious moments occur when you're just mucking around, washing the dishes, or painting your fence. Building an emotional relationship with your child is not the same as building a business relationship. Although studies on the relative importance of quality and quantity in parental contact with children are inconclusive,[3] time should be regarded as the primary ingredient of these relationships. In a world filled with people leading crowded lives, both quality and quantity of parental involvement are under threat.

DEALING WITH FAMILY BREAKDOWN

The ability of governments to intervene and foster more active, committed fathering is obviously limited. Making workplaces more family friendly will help, and education strategies can have some impact, but it's not possible to force fathers to engage more with their children.

There is, however, one parenting situation where the state already intervenes very heavily where these issues could be more seriously pursued. The way our society deals with children of failed marriages requires a serious rethink.

On most issues, politicians respond to whoever complains longest and loudest. The child support system is one glaring exception to this rule. With a few honourable exceptions, it seems that the more politicians are exposed to complaints about the system, the less they do about it. The issues involved are complex, extremely emotionally charged, and apparently intractable.

Over 700,000 Australian children are living with one parent only.[4] Some studies suggest that around 45 percent of children whose non-resident parent is still alive do not see that parent regularly.[5] In many cases, contact ceases completely. In the overwhelming majority of cases the absent parent is the father.

With nearly half of all marriages destined to end in divorce, this situation is now an entrenched feature of the Australian social landscape. Yet our society deals with the issues arising from family breakdown as matters which affect an unfortunate small minority who are essentially responsible for dealing with their own problems.

What are the typical consequences of family breakdown for a family with young children? Apart from the inevitable emotional trauma and consequential damage which often occurs, the lives of all those involved are changed dramatically. One parent, usually the mother, often acquires almost total responsibility for caring for the children. Even if the departing parent previously contributed little, the withdrawal of an adult from a household with children can have a big impact on the burden carried by the primary carer. This additional burden is usually accompanied by financial difficulties and changes to work arrangements. Sometimes financial difficulties will be even worse because of the departing parent can't or won't pay the appropriate level of child support.

The departing parent, usually the father, suffers the multiple shock of enforced separation from children, loss of income and assets through child support arrangements, and the need to establish a new household. If his work life is in any way unstable, insecure or stressful, these consequences are magnified.

The children of the marriage suffer the effective loss of a parent, which they sometimes interpret as abandonment. The emotional environment in which the children continue growing up changes. In some cases this change is for the better, as an environment of hostility, anger and even violence is dissolved. In many other instances the emotional challenges presented to children by the breakdown of their parents' marriage are substantial. Often these challenges are accompanied by changes in living standards, such as moving to new accommodation or having fewer resources for the essentials of life and small luxuries. No matter how financial obligations are structured, someone loses. In many cases, both parties suffer an effective loss of income and wealth.

Like virtually all of my colleagues I've dealt with the angry dads and desperate mums who typify the world of child support, and have felt unable to do anything useful to improve the system. For every angry dad I've encountered, mired in hopeless poverty and social isolation, I've dealt with an equivalent desperate mum, unable to get adequate child support from a conniving father and fighting endless battles within the child support system.

The typical reaction of angry men, and their myriad support groups, doesn't offer much of a solution to problems in the child support and family law systems. Their cause is often diminished by their vehemence and their inability to see the problems their ex-partner is facing. Almost by definition they tend to be the hard cases, men whose wives have left them and whose lives have been virtually crippled by financial and emotional loss.

The extreme nature of the attacks by some critics of the family law and child support systems shouldn't be allowed to blind us to the need for reform. When considered from a relational perspective, there are major issues which need to be addressed.

Having become a non-custodial parent myself, in circumstances thankfully well removed from those which characterise the more extreme cases, I can now draw on personal experience on these issues. Having thought about them a good deal, I believe there's a systemic weakness in the way our society approaches these problems. Relational analysis very quickly exposes the fundamental flaw in the child support system: it's almost totally about money.

In the 1980s, when less than a third of custodial parents received child support payments, thus exposing them and their children to serious poverty and the Government to mounting welfare bills, it was not surprising that the focus of reform was money. Today, however, underneath the continuing battles about how that reform is enforced lies a broader set of issues about human relationships and our responsibility to care for our children.

My greatest challenge as a non-custodial parent has been fulfilling my non-financial responsibilities as a father to my children. My greatest heartache has come from the experience of being a part-time parent and occasional visitor in my children's lives. Although I continue to sustain them financially, I'm a much more remote factor in their lives. Most of their small triumphs and disasters I'm unable to share. My ability to act as a positive influence in their lives is limited. My emotional bond with them is qualified because I'm not always there for them.

Sustaining and nurturing an emotional bond with small children for one weekend per fortnight is not easy. They're not surrounded by the familiar infrastructure of bedrooms, toys and personal belongings, but have only the pale version of these things I've managed to put together. My obligation to provide discipline is heavily qualified – if I chastise my daughter or deny my son a treat I risk spoiling my time with them. I don't necessarily have the time to allow their hurt feelings to recover.

Having grappled with these challenges, I find it disturbing that, according to the Australian Bureau of Statistics Family Characteristics Survey, 30 percent of children with separated parents have little or no contact with their non-custodial parent, and of those who have some contact, for more than 20 percent it's no more than once every one to three months.[6] A third of children who have contact with their non-custodial parent never stay overnight, which Institute of Family Studies research suggests is highly beneficial to building a strong relationship.[7] Although in some cases contact may be undesirable or impossible, the lack of any serious mechanism in the system to promote it is cause for major concern.

The child support and family law systems focus largely on financial rather than relational issues. The Child Support Agency is extremely vigilant in ensuring that my children continue to enjoy the benefit of my money, but essentially indifferent to their need to continue to enjoy my love.

Although the Family Law Act includes statements of parental responsibility for the upbringing of children, in practice the system tends to deal with parental contact with children of a past relationship as a question of rights, not responsibilities. Access issues often parallel property disputes, with children almost regarded as pieces of property that a non-custodial parent is entitled to use from time to time. There's little incentive for a separated parent to continue to provide parental care and attention to their children. There seems to be no penalty or sanction for those who fail to do so. As an absent father I'm given a choice whether to continue my relationship with my children, not an obligation.

If my former wife decides to move to Darwin, the law will take some account of the negative impact this would have on my ability to access my children, but also the likely effect on the children if their mother is prevented from moving. If I move to Perth, the dramatic reduction in my contact with my children will attract no sanction as long as I continue to pay my child support payments.

To take another example, a friend of mine has not seen her father since she was eight years old, the age my daughter is now. She feels the hurt of this abandonment very deeply. Yet our society thought nothing of it, provided the cheques kept rolling in until she was eighteen. I recently encountered a man who has left his wife and three small children, has seen his children once in three months, and plans to move interstate. Irrespective of the damage it causes to his children, our society will do nothing about his behaviour.

A RELATIONAL APPROACH

The question of access to children by a non-custodial parent should be primarily a matter of responsibility, not right. Our society should expect parents to continue to participate in the lives of their children after separation to the greatest extent possible. Parents should be obliged to accept that the constraints that having children imposes on their freedom of movement do not end when their marriage breaks down. Sharing of parenting responsibilities is the preferable approach to bringing up children, both within and beyond marital relationships. In some cases this won't be appropriate, such as when an abusive parent is involved, but wherever possible, some continued involvement should be expected of the non-custodial parent.

A genuine case management approach, built on a starting presumption of continued parental involvement, could enable such a change of emphasis to occur. More divorcing parents could be asked to develop a 'parenting plan' stating the responsibilities of both parents to participate in the ongoing nurturing of their children. Such plans are provided for in the existing system but are rarely used. If the fine words about continuing parental responsibility in the Family Law Act are to mean anything, the way the system operates must change.

It was once possible for all separating parents to make use of the Family Court counselling service. Now only those involved in legal proceedings can access the service. A potentially crucial mechanism for influencing the behaviour of separating parents has been removed. In a system genuinely concerned to ensure that wherever possible non-custodial parents continue to play a role in their children's upbringing, such counselling would be compulsory, not unavailable.

Academic studies indicate that the level of conflict between separated parents is a good indicator of how much involvement the non-custodial parent will have with their children – more conflict, less involvement, and vice versa.[8] Changing the system to place more emphasis on parental responsibilities will have little effect in cases of extreme conflict, and in cases of strong co-operation, because greater involvement will be very difficult to achieve in the former case and probably unnecessary in the latter. In most situations, however, it would introduce positive pressures calculated to increase parental involvement in the lives of their children.

Although some separated parents who have little or no contact with their children would perhaps be best left that way, it's hard to believe this should be the case for most of the almost 45 percent in this category.

The Family Court's response to these matters does not provide much cause for hope. In an extraordinary interview in *The Age* in September 2002, Chief Justice Alistair Nicholson expressed the view that separated fathers often seek more contact with their children for reasons of financial gain, and that any greater linkage between contact hours with children and the level of child support obligations would lead to a more litigious environment.[9]

Almost by definition the Family Court devotes most attention to the hardest cases. It's therefore understandable that the Chief Justice would overemphasise the extent and significance of particular kinds of misbehaviour, and downplay the enormous number of cases where it's unlikely to occur. The problem is, unfortunately, that the Family Court sets the benchmarks by which all separation and custodial arrangements are determined. If our approach to the question of greater involvement by separated parents in their children's lives starts not with the assumption that a child has an emotional right to that involvement, but with a presumption that such a responsibility would be exploited for financial gain, something is very seriously wrong.

It's widely believed that children from broken families are more likely to be involved in antisocial behaviour later in life. The nature of the causal connection continues to be a matter of highly charged debate, in which issues of poverty, race and gender figure prominently. Recent work by the New South Wales Bureau of Crime Statistics and Research suggests that poor parenting, rather than single parenting, is the causal link.[10] Family breakdown is still relevant however, because unless the departing parent's contribution was negative in overall terms, parenting is likely to become harder when only one parent remains to do it.

The nostalgic conservative response to this issue, stated most recently by Malcolm Turnbull in a speech at Sydney University, is to try to strengthen the institution of marriage and reduce the number of divorces.[11] This approach is destined to fail, and indeed to cause significant damage if it's ever applied properly, because it ignores the fundamental changes in our society that have led to the rapid increase in the level of family breakdown. Changes in the role of women in our society and in the shape and structure of our sexual relationships have been driven by changes in technology and the process of production, and these cannot be reversed. The overall life equation confronted by those contemplating marriage, having children, or divorcing is dramatically different from that which their grandparents faced. Most of the components of that equation can't be altered by governments without their being accused, rightly, of extreme social engineering.

A focus on relationships offers the prospect of common ground between conservative and progressive views on these issues. It would enable our society to promote long-term, stable and committed relationships without the authoritarian and discriminatory connotations associated with the conservative approach. A community divided by attitudes to marriage and family can unite around a commitment to stronger relationships.

We must accept that many of our society's children will be brought up in the absence of one of their natural parents, and seek to address the negative aspects of that situation without unduly interfering in people's personal lives. The 1980s reforms to the child support system sought to deal with the financial side of these problems. It's now time we tackled the emotional difficulties of family breakdown, and sought to minimise their negative consequences for the children involved. By placing human relationships at the front of our thinking, we can understand the problem very clearly. Our task is to reform the system so that it reinforces the parenting role of both parents in a broken marriage and ensures that, wherever possible, children continue to receive emotional as well as financial sustenance from a departed parent. Unlike other possible reforms, this new approach need not create any losers. Any minor additional incursions on the individual freedom of adults it may entail would be worth the individual benefit for our children and the broader relational benefit for our society.

It's time our society started to treat its responsibility for bringing up children differently, and moved beyond the individualistic and economic assumptions of the existing system. By dealing with these issues from a broader relational perspective, a very different approach would ultimately emerge. If we continue to deal with children as items on a family balance sheet, we won't address the problems in their relationships, or the consequential problems in their adult relationships when they grow up.

8

OUR AUSTRALIAN IDENTITY

Being an Australian, being a part of Australian society, and having a share in the Australian identity are all central to the relationships of each individual Australian. Who we are governs how we relate. Any discussion of relationships in our society would not be complete without examining our collective relationships with ourselves, which are mediated by a range of political, social and cultural institutions.

Relationships are about connection and common ground. Much of that common ground consists of our own sense of who we are, and the symbols that reflect our identity. Communities with a shared identity will relate much better than those divided by identity issues. 'Them and us' is the deadly enemy of better community relationships.

Our individual relationships are built around a complex framework of symbols and identities. The greater the underlying cohesion in this framework, the stronger those individual relationships will be. Over the past decade Australian identity has become a major political battle-ground. A series of conflicts around multiculturalism, Aboriginal reconciliation, our flag and the Republic have split the nation and our sense of common identity. It's almost as if there are now two Australias in the collective minds of its inhabitants, each aggressively asserting its own legitimacy and denying that of the other.

Debates about who we are, how we relate to each other and how we relate to the rest of the world are nothing new in Australia. In the 1920s our society was split around the theme of 'loyalty', which meant loyalty to a protestant God, the British Empire and the market. Catholics and trade unionists were excluded from this dominant definition of Australian identity and, naturally enough, they developed an alternative story.

Such struggles can be healthy if they remain peaceful, but they shouldn't be allowed to continue forever. In particular they should always be fought with the objective of inclusion, not exclusion, and winner-takes-all approaches should be avoided. Our collective identity is ultimately built on widespread legitimacy. Formally recognising a new symbol means little if it's not accepted as legitimate by half the population. Proponents of change in this area must always remember that such innovations are only successful when they change what's in people's hearts.

Movements to change our national identity and symbols – such as the campaigns for a new flag and a Republic – have struggled because they've been built more on repudiating our past than on imagining our future. Reactionary opponents of change have instinctively understood this, and zeroed in on the widespread sense among many Australians that somehow they're under attack for being who and what they are. Concepts like the 'black armband view of history' have been created to exploit this unease, and emphasise the sense of attack implied in such campaigns. People are understandably reluctant to sign up to propositions that imply repudiation of their own past identity. Hence many will resist the notion of saying sorry to Aboriginal people but readily accept the idea of 'practical reconciliation' promoted by John Howard, because it suggests tackling existing problems for which they have no direct responsibility and does not imply there's something wrong with them.

If we're genuinely to strengthen the relationship bonds in our society and move beyond the deep divisions in our identity, we need to rethink our approach to these issues. A little more persuasion, a little more sensitivity, and a little less belligerence would help to smoothe the path of necessary social changes. It might also help us see that there are some aspects of our old identity that should be accepted or even embraced, not rejected. Campaigns for change need to be pursued as a progression from our past, a building upon existing foundations, rather than a repudiation of the past. They must avoid the arrogance which so easily seeps into the demeanour and approach of the zealous reformer. Unless reformers are able to build an inclusive strategy for change, we're destined to fail, and to create bitter divisions which will bring out the worst of people on both sides of the debate.

WHATEVER HAPPENED TO THE REPUBLIC?

The failed campaign for a Republic is the primary example of this lesson. The entire campaign was built around overt repudiation of Australia's British origins, imposition of an unpopular model of presidential appointment, and overuse of celebrities and advertising hype.

As a person of British origin, with numerous British relatives and a deep love of British history and culture, I don't believe that establishing a truly unique Australian identity should be done at the expense of our deep and enduring links with Britain. Shallow bunyip nationalism and puerile pommy-bashing should have no place in the campaign for a Republic. We should be aiming to entrench our own Australian identity, not reject our British origins. Australia's Republic must be a positive expression of our unique national character and destiny, not a negative reaction to the connections of kinship, culture and history. We want to define ourselves by who we are, not by who we are not.

The significance of this point was brought home to me during the Republic campaign when a prominent legal academic once linked with Labor said to me: 'I simply cannot accept the notion of Britain as a foreign country.' Neither can I. I was brought up in the Anglican Church and my cultural and social outlook is dominated by British influences. I feel the same way about Britain as an Australian of Greek origin feels about Greece. As a majority of Australians are also of British origin, it's clear that any Republic built on the notion of Britain as a foreign country just like any other foreign country is destined to struggle for community acceptance.

The focus in the 1999 campaign on this more superficial aspect of

Australian nationalism meant that a more potent element of our traditional identity, our egalitarianism, was downplayed. Our future campaign for a Republic should be based on a collective commitment to genuine equality of opportunity in all areas of our society, not repudiation of our past.

It should be a core principle of our society that all positions in our system of government are open to all citizens, irrespective of birth, creed, race or gender. Any political office that involves the representation of citizens should be open to all those being represented.

This fundamental principle was established most firmly and profoundly during the French Revolution of 1789. It can be found in Article 6 of the Declaration of the Rights of Man and of the Citizen, adopted by the National Assembly of France on August 26, 1789:

> All citizens, being equal in the eyes of the law, are equally eligible
> to all dignities and to all public positions and occupations,
> according to their abilities, and without distinction except
> that of their virtues and talents.

This principle should be at the very heart of our system of government. If our society is to be built on the notion that we're all inherently equal and that we enjoy equal rights, opportunities and responsibilities, these principles must be reflected in the way we govern ourselves.

Monarchy infringes this principle. Any monarchy does. Determining our head of state by the accident of birth into a particular family is a relic of a medieval world, a world of short life expectancies, pervasive superstition and brutal living conditions. In such a world, where political conflict was invariably violent and bloody, the certainty and stability provided by the institution of monarchy made some sense. In a modern peaceful and democratic society it makes no sense at all. It's absurd that all Australian children can aspire to be our Prime Minister, but none can aspire to be our head of state.

The fact that our monarch is also monarch of various other countries merely reinforces this absurdity. Our national symbols should be uniquely Australian, and our national identity should be clear and unequivocal. Having the monarch of another country on the other side of the world as our head of state raises obvious questions about our independence, sovereignty and identity. These questions may be essentially symbolic rather than substantive, but they still carry meaning. There's an empty space at the centre of our national life and identity. No pictures of a unifying national leader adorn our nation's schoolrooms. The fifty-year-old photos of the Queen sometimes found in public halls and council chambers are embarrassing and a little bit pathetic.

It's now almost four years since the referendum defeat in 1999. It's an appropriate time for rethinking and regrouping. We need to reconsider the lessons of past experience and the scope of future opportunities. Our starting point must be to accept the umpire's decision. The Australian people rejected a Republic in 1999. We should not try to explain this away. We should accept it at face value.

This leads us to a simple conclusion. If a new proposal for a Republic is to succeed, it must be fundamentally different from the one rejected by the people in 1999. In particular, it must incorporate direct election of the president. The parliamentary appointment model is dead, and we shouldn't waste our energies trying to revive it.

The quality of relationships between citizens and governments in Australia has deteriorated markedly in recent decades. The referendum for a Republic presented an opportunity to address this problem. The sense of connection between governments and governed could have been enhanced. Instead the decline of our political relationships was ignored, and proposals were advanced that responded to problems many Australians regarded as of much lesser significance.

The rejection of the 1999 referendum was based on one dominant concern: political accountability. There's a widely held view in our community that our politicians and institutions are insufficiently accountable. Monarchists were able to harness this sentiment – 'Say No to the politicians' republic' – to defeat the referendum. In effect it became their only argument.

Much of the Republican debate consisted of arguments and concepts which run directly counter to this powerful community sentiment. Political insiders concentrated on developing models designed to ensure that a Republic would bring as little political change as possible. This was correctly interpreted by many voters as political elites seeking to insulate themselves from the threat of greater political accountability.

The McGarvie model of presidential appointment by a council of 'wise elders' was overtly elitist. Claims that direct election might lead to Kylie Minogue becoming president reflected a profound reluctance to trust the Australian people to elect their own leader. Even the Gallop model of direct election involved nomination by Parliament, thus keeping the process safely inside the realm of the political elite. The flavour of public debate was heavily tainted with disdain for anything involving greater accountability. Many Labor voters, whose support for a Republic was taken for granted, voted 'No' as a result. As a direct election supporter of long standing who nevertheless chose to vote 'Yes', I understand their decision to do so.

Any future Republican proposal which is not built on the theme of greater accountability will fail. Instead of starting with the primary aim of minimum change, we should pursue the core objective of maximum accountability. This means embracing direct election of the president and starting from scratch.

It means accepting that greater accountability is the price the community will demand for change, and that they're right to do so. Our new Republic must be primarily about democracy, not nationalism.

Although direct election raises a number of difficult issues, none are insurmountable. The challenge to create a more accountable Republican model can be met. Yet more is needed. For a new Republican campaign to succeed, it must be built on a renewed commitment to democracy and accountability and immersed in a spirit of positive nationalism which both offers a new direction for the future and embraces the symbols of the past. We must rethink our approach to a number of symbolic issues in order to bridge the deepening cultural divide and build a new Australia on the foundations provided by the old.

OUR NATIONAL SYMBOLS

Most aspects and symbols of our national identity are riven with doubt and division. Enthusiasm for our national anthem is still a bit lukewarm. Interest in our national day is perfunctory. Many would like to change our flag. Community opinion is ambivalent about critical aspects of our identity, such as our multicultural society and our continuing reliance on traditional powerful friends like Britain and the United States.

Debates about these issues have generally been conducted in isolation from each other and have been dominated by the usual suspects with fairly predictable positions. Some of these arguments are getting a little stale.

If we're to develop a society built on better relationships, dealing with these fundamental questions about who we are in a constructive and inclusive way is essential. If we're to overcome the division fostered and exploited by John Howard, our society has to approach these questions from a different standpoint, just as we need to elevate the Republican debate beyond its anti-British aspect.

Some may regard this as a rather embarrassing admission, but I quite like 'Advance Australia Fair'. Musically it is not as stirring as some anthems, but cursory viewing of the Olympics and the World Cup suggests that it's better than most. Its lyrics evoke many key aspects of our identity without being unduly bombastic or maudlin, and, most importantly, they're very inclusive. In the context of the culture wars over Australian identity, 'Advance Australia Fair' has something for everyone. Traditionalists rather like phrases like 'young and free' and 'wealth for toil', while progressives warm to 'for those who've come across the sea we've bounteous plains to share', particularly in our current political climate. Some see the lyrics as banal but, apart perhaps from 'our land is girt by sea', I think this criticism is unfair. 'Our land abounds in nature's gifts of beauty rich and rare' might seem mundane to some, but it reflects exactly how we're perceived in the rest of the world. The universal joke about people not knowing the words is less accurate than it once was, and to the extent that it's true, I think it reflects a typical Australian distaste for pomp and ceremony rather than a rejection of the song itself.

We should embrace 'Advance Australia Fair' as a major success story that is gradually achieving widespread acceptance throughout our community. No Australian, whether traditional conservative or progressive radical, should feel alienated by our national anthem. It's a good expression of who we are and how we see ourselves and relate to each other as individuals within a nation.

The question of our national day is more complex. In spite of recent attempts to hype it up, Australia Day remains a rather limp affair, little more than a public holiday for most Australians. It lacks direction and substance because the broader aspects of the event it commemorates, expansion of the British Empire, subjugation of Aborigines, and the establishment of a brutal penal colony, are not easy to celebrate. It can't be a genuinely inclusive event for these reasons. Any attempt to attribute meaning to Australia Day is doomed to fail, because the kind of spirit and values our society would like to promote have virtually no connection with the events of January 26, 1788.

The anniversary of Federation suffers from the fact that it's also New Year's Day, and that popular awareness of and interest in the formal creation of the Australian nation is rather limited. Public enthusiasm for the celebration of the centenary of Federation was rather modest.

The only day which can lay claim to being our real national day is Anzac Day. Once derided as a relic of a bygone era, Anzac Day has made a remarkable comeback in recent years. In particular, much of the antagonism towards it from the left seems to have softened. Militant anti-militarism of the 1970s driven by opposition to Australian involvement in Vietnam has matured into much greater acceptance of the legitimacy and importance of Anzac Day. Many on the left may not have exactly embraced Anzac Day, but it now enjoys a level of community acceptance and support that would have seemed impossible thirty years ago.

As part of the process of strengthening our national identity and the common bonds of relationship which underpin it, I believe we should accept Anzac Day as a genuinely national day which is capable of including all Australians. Although it has less direct significance for some sections of the community, it symbolises values relevant to everyone.

The notion that Anzac Day is somehow a celebration of jingoism, militarism and war is completely wrong. In fact, if you consider the facts in some detail, it's about as far from this as it's possible for any commemoration of a military battle to be.

The attack on Gallipoli was a disastrous defeat. It was organised by another nation, and Australia was one of several nations that suffered severe casualties. All the Australians involved were volunteers. It was part of a much broader conflict, in which Australia participated in numerous other theatres. It's commemorated jointly with another nation, New Zealand, and the bi-national nature of the event is even reflected in its name. The most enduring Australian icon of the Gallipoli campaign, Simpson and his donkey, is based on a non-combatant who was something of a radical. The campaign involved an enemy for whom Australians felt respect, not hatred, and with whom we had little real argument. The Australian Turkish community now runs Anzac Day commemorations as a means of honouring the sacrifice of all those who were involved.

Our society is slowly but surely uniting behind Anzac Day as our real national day, when we acknowledge the courage and self-sacrifice of many of our forebears and reflect on our own good fortune to be citizens of Australia. It evokes genuine deep emotion in a way that Australia Day never will. It's been the subject of many songs, books, films and stories, whereas Australia Day has been all but ignored. It's impossible to listen to the words of the ode from *For the Fallen* without being moved.

At his seventieth birthday celebration a few years ago, my father made a speech based on the theme that he'd been very lucky in life. He concluded by saying that, more than anything else, he had been lucky to be born Australian. As a person whose own father was wounded on the western front in World War I and many years later died from the effects of being gassed, he has a very strong awareness of how fortunate

Australia has become as a country. For him, and I think for the vast majority of Australians, Anzac Day serves as an ideal reminder of what a great country we belong to, and a recognition of the sacrifices made by many of our forebears to help make it that way. It symbolises self-sacrifice and service to the community. It allows the younger generation to say thank you to the older.

For me, Anzac Day is a powerful connection with two grandfathers I never knew. As a child my father would bring me to Melbourne to attend the Anzac Day march. I asked questions about my grandfathers, who both fought in World War I and suffered a great deal as a result. My sense of connection with the past was built on a collective commemoration of the sacrifice of many thousands of Australians, which enabled me to build relationships with two men I never met.

The fact that there are many Australians who can't share in such connections doesn't diminish the significance of the event. In a nation of immigration, there'll always be many citizens whose identity is defined by other stories. Provided that the themes of Anzac Day are universal and inclusive, this is no reason for downplaying the importance of the commemoration. Any national mythology will inevitably resonate more directly with some citizens than others.

The question of our flag is an even more vexed one. From a purely utilitarian perspective, it's hard to refute the case for change. Having the flag of another country in the corner, which also ensures that our flag is easily mistaken for that of various other mostly small and obscure nations, is not a desirable situation. For those who are not of British origin, it's not an inclusive symbol. For those who have reason to actively reject British rule, such as Aboriginal Australians and Irish Australians, it can even be offensive. The notion that Australians have fought *for* the flag is puerile. Our flag may have been a symbol under which Australian soldiers fought, but so were the British Empire and 'God Save the King'. Our soldiers were fighting for freedom and national preservation, not a flag.

However, the issue is not that simple. Our flag still enjoys widespread if not universal support, and the absence of an obvious alternative makes the case for change much more problematic. Every alternative design I've ever seen has left me completely cold, and some are so appalling that I wouldn't dream of supporting them. When the change from 'God Save the Queen' to 'Advance Australia Fair' occurred, our community was ready for change and had an identifiable alternative with fairly broad public acceptance to turn to. None of this is the case with our flag.

The presence of the Union Jack in our flag has more legitimacy than the British monarchy or 'God Save the Queen' because it's only part of the flag, and therefore can be legitimately regarded as a reflection of the dominant influence in our history, rather than the entirety of our identity. The use-by date of our flag is approaching, but there's no particular reason why we should try to hurry it along.

Australia does have another flag which has grown in recognition and which, unlike our national flag, is a spectacular design which superbly evokes the harsh beauty of our natural landscape. The Aboriginal flag has become a very powerful symbol which is starting to reflect a wider range of sentiments than just the essential identity of Aboriginal Australians. It's very unlikely that reconciliation between Aboriginal and non-Aboriginal Australia will reach a point where the Aboriginal flag could become Australia's national flag. However, this flag is likely to continue to grow in status and, if nothing else, will be a powerful counterpoint to any proposed design for a new national flag. Its success should remind us that changing our flag will only be possible if we have a new design with widespread popular acceptance. Popular support for changing our flag will emerge only towards the end of the broader evolutionary changes in our national identity. It will only prevail when there's an identifiable alternative. Rather than engage in a futile search for a new symbol, we would be better to allow events to take their course. In the absence of a strong and widely accepted alternative to our existing flag, I see no reason why we need to tear it down. We must seek improvement, not repudiation, if we are to build a strong, more inclusive Australian identity.

BEYOND CULTURE WARS

One of the reasons for approaching these issues about national symbols with a constructive rather than belligerent tone is that these debates can impede progress in matters of much greater substance, such as multiculturalism and Aboriginal reconciliation. If those promoting change are able to seek more common ground with those resisting it, the prospects for change in how we treat people of different backgrounds will improve significantly. It's when such causes get confused with an assault on traditional values and attitudes that they encounter deeper resistance. If the battle to strengthen multiculturalism is wrapped up in a campaign to change the flag, for example, changing community attitudes will be a good deal harder.

Strengthening multiculturalism is an essential requirement for developing better relationships in Australian society. We grow through relationships with people who are different from us. Established citizens and newcomers discover they have more in common than they thought, and each changes the other in small and subtle ways. If each person feels included in our society and each culture is allowed social space in which to exist and evolve, the outcome is a more robust, vibrant and diverse community built on mutually rewarding relationships both within and across cultures. Interaction between indigenous and non-indigenous Australians is the most important sphere in which strengthening relationships across cultures will benefit our society. Progressive Australians committed to these causes have been taught a few lessons by John Howard recently. It's essential that these lessons are absorbed and understood.

Those of us committed to causes like multiculturalism and Aboriginal reconciliation have spent far too much time talking to each other, and too little time engaging with the broader community. When this engagement does occur, although it's generally constructive, there's often an element of hectoring which provides the forces of conservatism with just enough ammunition to persuade nervous and sceptical Australians that what they're facing is an assault on their values and identity.

While racism is a very substantial element in the backlash against such campaigns, it's by no means the only element. We should be able to separate out the legitimate concerns from the racist sentiments, and deal with those concerns on their merits. If we don't do this, we have little chance of changing the community sentiment which has been so carefully fostered and manipulated by the Howard Government.

Our ability to deepen and strengthen the web of relationships in our community depends to a great extent on making multiculturalism and Aboriginal reconciliation work. If we fail, we face the prospect of a society based on 'relational apartheid', full of racial and cultural divisions built on fear, hatred and contempt. That's why the struggle over our national identity and national symbols is so important, and why it can't be approached from a winner-takes-all perspective. Those who preach inclusion must also practise it.

Literally universal acceptance of a national symbol is impossible to achieve. Unless that symbol is completely devoid of meaning, it must inevitably contain within it the seeds of disagreement and controversy. The challenge for our society is to achieve some level of resolution of the endless battles over our own identity, and seek to mould the better elements of the old and new into a stronger, more unifying community identity.

Moving beyond the culture wars of the past fifteen years is critical to revitalising relationships within our community. The greater the common ground between people of different backgrounds, values and aspirations, the greater the capacity for building productive and healthy relationships across those community divisions. Our relationships with each other will be strengthened if they're built on the shared terrain of an inclusive national identity. Those of us who are initiators of change have a profound responsibility to ensure that we pursue change in an inclusive and understanding way.

9

DIGITAL RELATIONSHIPS

Information technology is changing the way we relate to each other more dramatically than we realise. From the personal to the global, the structure of our relationships is being reconfigured by technological change. Although much of the impact of this change is positive, it does have seriously negative aspects. We may not be able to halt the march of technology, but we do have choices about how we use it. The health and strength of our relationships should be a critical factor in such choices.

THE LIBERATING POWER OF TECHNOLOGY

Liberation from the landline and the letter, by mobile phone and email, has completely changed the way we relate to each other. The tyranny of time and space has been largely conquered. As these two technologies gradually merge and Internet use is elevated to an entirely new level by broadband access, we're entering an 'always on' world where visual, verbal and written communications know few limitations.

When I was growing up in East Gippsland, long-distance calls to relatives in Melbourne and Brisbane were expensive, and calls to our cousins in England were a very occasional luxury which had to be rationed. Now I can call or email my English relatives at a cost barely greater than the real price of a local call when I was a child.

The communications revolution has expanded our horizons far more than we realise. We can now stay in touch with friends and acquaintances no matter where they are. A former work colleague of mine who is studying overseas sends broadcast emails to a wide range of his Australian friends and contacts, thereby effectively remaining in touch with minimal effort. Recently I used email to track down a childhood friend from my short time living in England, an American boy with whom I had had no contact for 35 years. We engaged in an extended email catch-up session over several months. For several years I ran an email chat list about contemporary political issues, which attracted participants from all over Australia and even a few from Europe. To organise them all into a discussion in one location would have been impossible. I've since met several of the contributors, and continued to discuss and debate issues with them.

The mobile phone has a similarly liberating effect. Meeting up with friends at the football is nowhere near as complicated as it used to be. I can return calls while driving home from work, hands-free of course. I can negotiate the details of tonight's dinner while I'm in the supermarket shopping. I'm infinitely more contactable for anyone who wishes to contact me, and voicemail and text messaging add the option of highly efficient one-way communication. If some of my mates want to gloat about Essendon's latest defeat without being interrupted by a return blast they can, and unfortunately they do.

The Internet offers opportunities to find information and people. It opens up exciting new possibilities in fields like genealogy, enabling people to research their own family histories. It enables virtual conversations which, because of distance or the number of participants, would be physically impossible. Most importantly of all, it allows like-minded people to communicate much more easily. If you were the only American history buff in a small town, before the Internet your ability to interact with fellow enthusiasts was very restricted. Now you can talk to virtually all of them throughout the entire world. Even the barriers of language are being broken down by instant translation technologies.

New technologies have opened up new opportunities for communications between elected representatives and the people they represent. Over the past few years I've received far more emails than letters from concerned citizens. The ease of email breaks down formality. I often receive emails which consist of a single sentence, like 'say no to war on Iraq'. I've never received a letter like that. Email is a much more conversational medium, a bit like bumping into someone in the street.

The world of the written word is also being transformed. Books, magazines and articles are no longer obscure and hard to find. I can access an almost infinite array of written material without leaving my office. I can send large quantities of written material to a friend or colleague instantly and at minimal cost.

THE LIMITS OF TECHNOLOGY

We don't yet appreciate how dramatic are the changes to our lives brought by these new technologies. They seem incremental, but no doubt the advent of the first horseless carriages did too. We particularly don't realise just how much they're altering the way we relate to each other.

The nature and shape of our relationships is changing subtly in response to the impact of these new technologies. We're spreading ourselves around more thinly, as we engage in relationships with a much wider range of people. We have much less undivided attention to offer any one person. Our need for time out to 'get away from it all' is steadily increasing. Our closest and deepest relationships are being eroded by a rising tide of wider personal interaction, and by isolating involvement with individual technologies. Our crowded lives are cluttered with contact but diminishing in connection.

My mobile phone might help me stay in touch, but it also interrupts face-to-face conversation and personal interaction. Such interruptions quickly degrade the quality of this personal contact. They put some of us in a state of permanent distraction, with two or three conversations occurring almost simultaneously. Mobile phones can seriously detract from the quality – and quantity – of time we spend with our children. When we answer, we're sending a subtle message that the importance of our time together is only conditional. The same applies to a conversation, outing or meal with a friend, relative, colleague or lover.

Some of the most seductive of the new technologies do not involve expanding our ability to communicate with other people, but rather entail building a deep relationship with an inanimate object. Computer games and some kinds of Internet use can be extremely isolating. It's not uncommon for both children and adults to devote large quantities of time to their computer, at the expense of broader social interaction.

My two children have recently acquired Gameboys. I now face a constant battle to limit their use while the kids are in my care. As a former electronic games enthusiast I understand how addictive they can be. Although they're extremely entertaining and help children develop their reflexes and motor skills, they can be extraordinarily socially isolating. When I take my children over to their cousins' house to play, I refuse to let them take their Gameboys in with them, for fear they'll simply sit there zapping electronic baddies and ignoring their cousins. Time that might otherwise be spent in play that develops their imaginations and social skills would be eaten up by a one-dimensional, mechanical activity which involves no relating with other human beings. A large proportion of our nation's children now have televisions or computers in their bedrooms, and are therefore more susceptible to withdrawal from such relational activities. Parental guidance is still the critical factor in how these technologies are used by children, but in a world where parents are under increasing stress the temptation to allow electronic gadgets to babysit children can be overpowering.

The world of the Internet can be lonely or social, depending on the user's choice. The social Internet, the domain of chat rooms and bulletin boards, has developed its own social etiquette which parallels that which governs our behaviour in the physical world. Superficially, relationships over the Internet resemble our other relationships. We seek out like-minded people, avoid people we don't like, exchange serious and trivial thoughts, and develop close personal relationships, even marriages.

Yet even though information technology enables us to relate to many more people with fewer physical constraints, these relationships remain fundamentally different from our relationships in the physical world.

Even contact by videoconference is fundamentally different from, and much narrower than, face-to-face contact. Body language, facial expression and tone of voice are means of human communication that often dominate our interaction with each other. I can't raise an eyebrow by email. I can't smile by mobile phone. I can't hug someone by videoconference.

BETTER RELATIONSHIPS THROUGH TECHNOLOGY

How, then, are our relationships affected by both the liberating and restrictive aspects of information technology? It has certainly opened up new means of communication that enable us to communicate with a much larger number of people, in a much wider array of circumstances. Some argue that future developments in technology will usher in a world that will be like having the entire human race in the same room.[1] Technology has enhanced our ability to relate to more of our fellow human beings enormously, and the positive effects of this cannot be underestimated. Our capacity to sustain existing relationships and build new ones has also been enormously increased by information technology.

At the same time, however, more loneliness and isolation can result from excessive use of the Internet or electronic games, which enable us to retreat into our own world, unencumbered by the need to relate to others. Activities that once provided the basis for conversation and informal interaction, like food preparation, have been taken over by technologies like the microwave oven. Because relationships usually need a context in which to flourish, removing the context provided by a communal or family activity ultimately undermines these relationships.

It's conceivable that as we exploit the ever-growing opportunities offered by information technology, the amount of 'face time' we spend with our loved ones will diminish. If our children are always available via their mobile phones, the practical factors of supervision and contact which force us to interact in person with them decrease. The availability of email conversation with a friend can tend to reduce the sense of need to catch up for a coffee. We're at risk of entering a world where our behaviour is characterised by continuous partial attention, where we are constantly interrupted, easily distracted and less deeply connected with others. When a friend of mine sent me an 'it's a boy!' text message recently it was not quite the same as a phone call, which in turn is not as emotionally connecting as direct personal contact.

Concerns are already emerging about the potentially corrupting influence of text messaging shorthand on teenagers' written language skills, the use of text messaging for bullying and harassment purposes, and even the threat of repetitive strain injury.

Information technology also threatens our privacy and personal security. The accumulation of personal information, and the tracking of our activities and location it entails, is already starting to undermine our sense of personal space. Having the entire human race in one room also means everyone can see and hear everything you do and say.

The recent resurgence of community concern about Internet pornography highlights another challenge presented by the information technology revolution. Regulatory arrangements for the traditional media are not perfect, but they do make it difficult for children to access hard-core pornography and they minimise accidental exposure. In the online world the seriously disgusting and offensive is as accessible as the merely titillating. Accidental or casual exposure to the most extreme material is almost routine.

Like so many of its other initiatives, the Howard Government's approach to this issue is all about being seen to do something, not about solving the problem. Its Internet censorship regime is ineffective, and although better education of parents about filtering technologies will help, stronger action may be required if the Internet industry refuses to take action itself. This is happening in some instances, such as popular search engine LookSmart screening out pornographic sites from the sites it directs users to. No-one wants to shackle the Internet as several authoritarian regimes have sought to do, but protecting children from really extreme pornography is an entirely appropriate justification for intervention. The anything goes ethos which permeates the online world is simply not acceptable in this context.

The globalising impact of information technology is generating equivalent challenges at a global level. It is enormously powerful and liberating, enabling us to break down barriers of distance, language and culture. It allows international dialogue between ordinary citizens, when such dialogue was once largely the preserve of governments and ruling elites. It has permitted the emergence of global public opinion and mobilisation of global forces of protest. It has allowed countless people to pursue and debate issues in their own country with a much deeper awareness of what is occurring on these issues in other countries.

Yet at the global level the march of information technology also has a downside. As the international dominance of English grows rapidly, thousands of languages face a longer-term threat of extinction. Already some tribal languages are disappearing. Globalisation threatens even national languages, particularly those spoken by small numbers of people in countries susceptible to global influences. It took centuries of English dominance to relegate Gaelic and Welsh to the status of minor languages in their own lands. Globalisation threatens to repeat this process across the world within decades.

The homogenisation of culture is also a feature of globalisation transmitted mostly by information technology. Whether this pheno-menon destroys many more fragile traditional cultures, or merely makes them more accessible to other cultures, is yet to be seen. The inherent contradiction in globalisation is described very effectively by Thomas Friedman in *The Lexus and the Olive Tree*.[2] Ancient and distinctive cultures are threatened by their people's desire for western living standards, which inevitably come with western cultural norms attached. How to overcome this contradiction is the central challenge facing many nations and peoples throughout the world.

The new technologies changing our world are overwhelmingly positive forces, but they carry significant challenges to the strength and health of our relationships. We should not oppose or resist them for that reason, but rather seek to manage or regulate their use to protect and enhance our relationships with each other. Just as we modify new technologies for reasons of safety, we should also consider their impact on our relationships. This does not necessarily mean intervention by governments, but it does require public recognition of the implications of changes to the way we communicate and interact with each other. In some cases, like the development of 'netiquette' on the Internet, people manage the use of technology in a relationships-friendly way by modifying their own behaviour. We need to show vigilance and understanding if the dazzling new technologies which are transforming our society are to enhance, not undermine, our capacity to relate to each other as human beings.

10

HUMANITY AND RELATIONSHIPS

The most fundamental relationship under challenge in the modern world is our relationship with ourselves, our shared humanity. We're entering a world in which the prospect of dramatic changes to the nature of human beings no longer lies only in the realm of science fiction. Politicians throughout the developed world are now beginning to face choices which may ultimately change the core characteristics common to all human beings, and thereby the nature of our relationships with each other.

An early glimpse of these dilemmas emerged in the parliamentary debate on euthanasia in 1996. The underlying question in this debate – should we allow human beings to kill each other in certain circumstances – parallels the emerging conundrums created by advances in biotechnology and nanotechnology. The views of the many participants in this debate were echoed later in the more recent debate on stem cell research and cloning. The difficult challenge of making decisions that require us to define the nature of our own humanity is effectively the same in each case.

THE RIGHT TO DIE?

I don't support voluntary euthanasia because I believe it would erode the fabric of our shared humanity, and introduce a different system of values into our relationships with each other and our relationships with our collective selves in the form of the state.

There are situations where death is inevitable, the person concerned is suffering extreme pain and desires death, and a medical professional assists them to die. In a narrow sense it's difficult to condemn that action as morally wrong. We routinely kill suffering animals to put them out of their misery, including animals we refuse to eat. The notion that ending suffering and making an inevitable death less prolonged and painful is somehow morally reprehensible is not an easy one for us to embrace.

Yet there's a different and much broader issue at stake, the question of whether society as a whole should legalise and formalise such acts of mercy. In the web of relationships in which our species exists, the taking of a human life is the ultimate evil act. To empower the state to authorise the taking of life would undermine the value we collectively give to human life, would lead to some lives being taken by mistake, and would require drawing artificial definitions and boundaries that would be impossible to maintain over time.

Legalising voluntary euthanasia suggests that the life of a person who is dying is worth little. It invites us to develop an informal hierarchy of importance for different human lives, in which some people are more worth saving than others. Although individuals have faced diabolical choices of this kind throughout human history, where for example the life of a mother or her baby can be saved but not both, it's a very different matter for the state to formalise the notion that some lives are less worth saving.

The subtle restructuring of our values which would flow through the web of human relationships would eventually affect the way we deal with situations involving life and death issues. Whether it's a government or a hospital making resource allocation decisions or an individual contemplating risking his or her life to save a drowning person who has terminal cancer, the implied devaluation of human life would flow through our values system, with no way of determining the magnitude or extent of the effects. Our ability to dissuade people from committing suicide would be significantly undermined. Subtle pressures on terminally ill people who do not want to die would emerge.

The fact that the people involved are extremely ill and suffering enormous pain makes the idea of 'voluntary' less certain, and could lead to deaths that are neither genuinely desired nor even inevitable. A mistaken diagnosis may be at the heart of a decision to die. A desire not to be a burden on relatives, or pressure from family members anxious to maximise their forthcoming inheritance, could affect the decision.

Whenever matters of life and death are under consideration, we should be particularly aware of human fallibility. Most western societies have abolished capital punishment because mistakes made in sentencing cannot be reversed. And although legalised euthanasia would be supposedly voluntary and governed by strict safeguards, there've been cases of people confessing to murders they didn't commit, being executed and later being exonerated when it was too late. Timothy Evans confessed to murdering his wife in Britain in the early 1950s, and was hanged. It was later discovered that the murder, along with numerous other murders, was committed by John Christie, and that police pressure, guilt about helping to dispose of his wife's body, and having subnormal intelligence had led Evans to confess to a crime he did not commit.[1]

Setting the boundaries on exactly who has access to assisted suicide is also worrying. There's no logical reason why it should be restricted to the terminally ill. The severely disabled, or those with degenerative diseases that will ultimately kill them, may be entitled to claim an equal right to die. The guardian of a child who's terminally ill and suffering extreme pain may, on behalf of the child, seek the right to let them die. Like our constant resort to drugs as an instant solution to difficult problems, voluntary euthanasia offers a superficial solution to an extremely complex problem.

THE MARCH OF SCIENCE

At the heart of this debate lie fundamental questions about the nature of our own humanity and the relational bonds which combine us all into a vast interconnected web of human relationships. Even an apparently limited change such as legalising voluntary euthanasia would reverberate throughout this complex system in ways which are not easy to predict over the longer term. The relational consequences of more fundamental changes to our species arising from biotechnology and other scientific advances are likely to be even more profound.

The challenges we face from technologies that have the potential to change who we are therefore are extraordinarily difficult. Most active participants in public debate don't seem to recognise just how central to the shape of our common future these issues are.

The use of embryonic stem cells for experimental purposes and the possible cloning of human beings, the subject of recent prolonged debate in the Federal Parliament, are just a couple of items on a rapidly growing list of scientific innovations that challenge the understood boundaries of our humanity.

Work involving building computers with organic materials such as light-emitting polymers, creating new organisms that never previously existed, growing biopharmaceuticals in animals, altering chemical imbalances in the human brain, and connecting all computers into a giant information ecosystem, contains the seeds of fundamental change to human existence. Scientists involved in robotics and artificial intelligence are already debating definitions for distinguishing human beings from robots, and questioning whether there is anything 'special' or 'unique' about human life that requires protection from unregulated scientific advancement.[2] Sun Microsystems co-founder Bill Joy, one of the great visionaries of the information revolution, even worries that the combined revolution in genetic engineering, nanotechology and robotics could effectively make human beings extinct.[3] Decades earlier, Christian ethicist C.S. Lewis speculated that the advance of technology may ultimately lead to the 'abolition of man'.[4]

Although the technical and scientific barriers to these more lurid possibilities are formidable, we can't assume that they are insurmountable.

Similar possibilities for changing the nature of our species arise from rapidly growing life expectancy and the prospect that science may deliver the means to obtain quasi-immortality. Even the major shift in the balance between young and old in western societies which is already well underway is beginning to alter the nature of our relationships. The longer we can live, the more risk-averse we're likely to become. History suggests that human life is cheap when it's short. Young men expecting to die in their thirties are much more likely to risk death in war than those with a life expectancy of eighty. Even the incremental advance of medical science and technology, and the enormous prolongation of life that may result, will bring about major changes in human relationships. A major debate is already emerging about whether insurance companies should have access to individual genetic information. If such material becomes accessible, the entire structure of life, health and disability insurance will change. The system of pooling risk between the fortunate and the less fortunate will be undermined.

The implications for the future of human life as we know it lying beneath the possibilities opened up by science go to the very heart of our concept of humanity. Our great challenge is that any decision to restrict or inhibit scientific and technological change almost inevitably establishes arbitrary and illogical lines that are unlikely to meet the test of time.

I accept the view that human life commences at birth, not conception. I also acknowledge that this is a socially imposed decision, in which our society collectively decides to attribute certain rights to 'fully-formed' humans and another set of rights to humans in embryonic form. Although I support the view that human life begins at birth, I also accept that there are very serious ethical issues associated with how we deal with human embryos and foetuses and the extent to which we allow any interference with the natural process of human procreation.

The emergence of in vitro fertilisation (IVF) in the 1980s opened up a set of ethical questions that are still prominent in debates about the future of human life. Once our society permitted IVF, it eventually had to confront the prospect of it being used by women without male partners, and the possibility of spare embryos otherwise destined for destruction being used for scientific experimentation. From this position it's a very short step to a situation where embryos are actually created for the purpose of experimentation rather than procreation.

Soon we may face choices about cloning, choosing the characteristics of babies in advance, creating hybrids with other species like chimpanzees, implanting organically based micro-computers in our bodies, using genetic engineering to eliminate hereditary diseases and disabilities, and employing neuropharmacology to permanently alter our personality characteristics. The prospect of dramatic improvement in the human condition will be offered through scientific advances that fundamentally change the nature of our humanity.

The universality of human dignity is threatened by the unimpeded march of science. If the bonds of shared humanity are loosened, notions of universal human equality will be undermined. The beautiful and the ugly, the intelligent and the unintelligent, the strong and the weak, all manage to co-exist in our society because they implicitly understand that each is that way through genetic chance. Where such human characteristics are artificially created, the divisions between those who possess them and those who don't may harden into faultlines of serious social conflict.

PRESERVING OUR HUMAN ESSENCE

The emerging debate about the future of humanity reflects an interminable tension between two competing approaches to questions of human life and progress, the spiritual view and the utilitarian view. This tension is at its peak in arguments around concepts like human nature and human dignity. These philosophical debates go back as far as Aristotle, who argued that our notions of right and wrong emerge from our own natures, and therefore our own natural desires, instincts and behaviour govern our approach to issues of moral judgment.[5]

These questions are explored with great insight by Francis Fukuyama in his recent book *Our Posthuman Future*.[6] Fukuyama argues that recent advances in biotechnology 'mix obvious benefits with subtle harms in one seamless package'. The potential harm that most threatens us is acquiring the ability to re-engineer human life, to change the nature of our characteristics, personalities and how we relate to each other, and ultimately to change the nature of what human beings are.[7]

Biology has shaped us, and changes in our biology will change us. Imagine a human society in which procreation no longer involves sex, or the maternal instinct is eliminated, or all people are of very similar height, and some of the possible consequences of changing our biology emerge. Already some fairly crude changes are in the system, waiting to take full effect. The deliberately engineered gender imbalance in some parts of China and India, where in some age groups there are more than 115 males for every female, are a biological time-bomb.

Fukuyama argues that science is in the process of empowering humanity to move to a 'posthuman' stage of evolution. He contends that human nature exists as a meaningful concept, and that it has provided a stable continuity to our experience as a species.[8]

I too believe that there is such a thing as human nature. I believe there are such things as human dignity and common humanity, and that they define and govern our relationships with each other. Our shared behavioural characteristics, even those which produce negative or antisocial outcomes, should not be tampered with lightly. Just as we have an obligation to future generations to ensure they inherit a sustainable environment, we also have an obligation to ensure that they inherit our characteristics as human beings. Our legitimate goal of guaranteeing biodiversity for future generations should extend to our own species.

The notion that the march of science is irresistible, and therefore all attempts to regulate or impede these scientific revolutions are ultimately futile, is misconceived. Regulation doesn't need to be absolutely perfect to be effective, nor does it necessarily entail outright prohibition. To be effective, regulation will require the input and agreement of mainstream scientists in the relevant fields, who must ultimately carry the responsibility on behalf of society at large of policing the activities of their less responsible colleagues. This dialogue between scientific leaders and the broader community is central to regulating and managing the process of scientific inquiry that may alter the human species.

The contribution to these debates from the churches should be valued, not spurned. Although our society may feel compelled to take positions on these issues which are at odds with the views of some churches, as it has done on IVF and embryonic stem cell research, the churches bring a vital perspective to the debate. Often the various mainstream churches themselves have different views on these highly contentious issues. Yet without the benefit of independent spiritual perspectives which focus on broader questions about the nature of human life, our society may drift into a mindlessly utilitarian position with potentially very serious and unpredictable longer-term consequences. Even when we disagree with a particular religious contribution on these issues, that contribution should still be valued.

As with the debate about euthanasia, the arguments surrounding biotechnology and genetic engineering are all built on the competing forces of individualism and society. Arguments for voluntary euthanasia, or unrestricted scientific advance, are based on notions of individual rights and freedoms. Opposing arguments are built on concerns for the longer-term consequences for all individuals, our relationships with each other, and society as a whole.

The notion of an individual right to experiment or a freedom to reproduce in any way desired is a false one. Notwithstanding worthy efforts by some philosophers to demonstrate the contrary, all our notions of human rights and freedoms are based on our understanding of human nature. Just as we restrict the right of an individual in order to protect other rights held by other individuals, it's only logical we should put limits on scientific inquiry or reproductive experimentation in order to protect other rights, including those of future generations.

Because it's not realistic to organise human society exclusively around either spiritual or utilitarian principles, the outcomes of future debates on these issues will inevitably be messy. Arbitrary restrictions will be imposed, illogical lines will be drawn and science will continue to advance haphazardly. Our most critical need is to understand the paramount importance of human relationships, and to ensure that the unique nature of how we relate to each other is not radically changed by scientific innovations intended to deliver other benefits. Preserving the essence of our own humanity is set to become a new frontier of global political conflict, perhaps even transcending the global battle to preserve and protect our environment. As in the case of the environment, we must accept that some change involving some cost is probably unavoidable. Yet we must also recognise that, as with the environment, the prospect of the ultimate destruction of the human species is a real one.

CONCLUSION – PUTTING RELATIONSHIPS AT THE CENTRE

Humans are social beings. Our lives have meaning essentially in the context of our relationships with other human beings.

Recent decades of economic progress have placed more and more stress on the quality and extent of our relationships. We work harder and longer, enjoying the fruits of choice but paying an indirect price as the web of social obligations underpinning our relationships unravels. Our relationships are becoming more and more conditional.

Until the 1960s the guiding story of advanced western societies was material well-being. Even the most economically and technologically advanced nations still carried the scars of war and depression, and, by today's standards, most people lived fairly basic lives. Economic progress was the totally dominant goal of society.

In the late 1960s an amalgam of personal fulfilment and individual freedom emerged as another guiding story. For many younger people who'd never known depression or war, other issues became more central. Concern for our broader physical environment also emerged as a driving force in social discourse. Gradually the dominance of economic progress as our community's guiding story was modified.

These changes have now been absorbed, yet the older guiding story is still with us. Certainly in the political arena the ideal of economic well-being and advancement seems no less powerful than it was several decades ago.

A new change is now underway, and the elements of a new guiding story are beginning to emerge. Like previous changes, it will modify, but not displace, the dominant economic orientation of our society.

That new guiding story deals with the strength and quality of our relationships. It incorporates many emerging contemporary issues like work and family and parenting. It raises issues that are difficult to grapple with in our existing political culture.

The nature of our political discourse must change in order to accommodate these changes in our society. Just as the environment has become central in political debate, so too must our relationships. We might manage to protect our physical environment, but that will advance our society little if we're laying waste to our emotional environment.

Our decision-making should incorporate relationship impact assessments. We should use relational audits as a means of examining the impact of government decisions on our relationships. The new outcomes framework in the Federal Budget process should be developed to incorporate analysis of the relationship outcomes of government decisions.

A little while ago I discovered quite by chance that an old friend of mine had become a father for the second time. His new baby was already nine months old. I was horrified to realise that I had grown so distant from someone I'd shared houses with, even written a book with, and who I still considered to be a good friend. It made me think about my relationships, and the negative effects of our high speed society.

The positive aspect of the story, however, was that my friend had taken twelve months off work to care for his children. My priorities might be open to challenge, but he at least was achieving some balance in his life.

Unfortunately, too few Australians are able to make such choices, because as a society we undervalue the importance of human relationships. Our crowded lives are gradually shredding our relationships with each other. Until we change our way of thinking, the pressures on our relationships will only get worse.

Relationships should be at the forefront of the new guiding story in our society. Our collective response to the major challenges we face must be based on our commitment to sustaining strong, healthy relationships and ensuring that all Australians have somewhere to belong in our society. We can move beyond entrenched divisions to tackle serious issues like parenting, youth alienation, crime, national identity, technology and family breakdown if relationships are placed at the centre of our thinking.

The depth and quality of our human relationships determines the strength of our society and the quality of our lives. It's time to put relationships at the centre of political debate. We can reignite the hope that is so vital to social and economic progress, and heal the divisions crippling our efforts to build a more cohesive and inclusive society. Building stronger relationships is the key to creating a better society.

REFERENCES

2 ALONE IN THE CROWD

1. Clive Hamilton argues that relationships are the most important determinant of human happiness: Hamilton, C. (2003) *Growth Fetish*, Allen & Unwin, Sydney, pp.35-39. He cites research (at p.69) that suggests there's a direct inverse correlation between the health of an individual's relationships and the extent to which they crave self-legitimising consumer goods and status symbols: Csikszentmihalyi, M. & Rochberg-Halton, E. (1981) *The Meaning of Things: Domestic Symbols and the Self*, Cambridge University Press, Cambridge, p.164.
2. Speech by Michael Schluter at Ridley College, Melbourne, 30 July 2001.
3. Schluter, M. & Lee, D. (1993) *The R Factor*, Hodder & Stoughton, London.
4. ibid., pp.36 et seq.
5. ibid.
6. ibid., pp.6 et seq.
7. Tanner, L. (1984) 'Working Class Politics and Culture: A Case Study of Brunswick in the 1920s', Master of Arts thesis, University of Melbourne, Melbourne, pp.40 et seq.
8. Sennett, R. (1998) *The Corrosion of Character*, W.W. Norton & Co, New York, pp.15 et seq. and pp.64 et seq.
9. Reich, R. (2001) *The Future of Success*, Alfred A. Knopf, New York, pp.196-207.
10. Bunker, S. et al. (2003) '"Stress" and coronary heart disease: Psychosocial risk factors', *Medical Journal of Australia*, vol.178, March 2003, p.272.
11. Mackay, H. (1997) *Generations: Baby Boomers, Their Parents and Their Children*, Macmillan, Sydney, p.82.

12. Schluter & Lee, op. cit., p.268.

13. Further information on the relational audit approach can be found in Schluter, M. & Lee, D. (2003) *The R Option*, Relationships Foundation, Cambridge, pp.55 et seq., and in Ashcroft, J. (2003) *Relationships: An Agenda for Change*, Relationships Foundation, Cambridge, p.18.

14. Schluter & Lee, *The R Factor*, op. cit., pp.68 et seq.

15. Speech by Schluter, 30 July 2001, op. cit.

16. Discussion with the author, 5 November 2002.

17. The Groom Government in Tasmania created a Family Unit in the public service to undertake family impact statements with respect to legislative proposals. See for example parliamentary debate on this issue in *Hansard*, House of Assembly, Vol.XV (1), 2 March to 1 April 1993, pp.253-256.

18. The structure of the Federal Budget is now notionally framed around outputs and outcomes. In essence, outputs represent activities and outcomes represent objectives. In theory the outcomes should encompass an element of benchmarking and measurement. In practice, however, they are still only very broad and rudimentary.

19. See Parliamentary Library brief, 'Corporate Performance – Triple Bottom Line', Canberra, 1999.

3 BEYOND LIBERATION

1. Clive Hamilton also acknowledges the dominance of individualism in the sixties revolution: *Growth Fetish*, op. cit., p.110.

2. Mackay, op. cit., pp.16-20.

3. Rawls, J. (1999) *A Theory of Justice*, Harvard/Belknap, Cambridge, pp.347-365.

4. Dworkin, R. (2000) *Sovereign Virtue: The Theory and Practice of Equality*, Harvard University Press, Cambridge, Massachusetts, p.324 et seq.

5. Sen, A. (1992) *Inequality Re-examined*, Clarendon Press, Oxford, pp.35-55.

6. Bowles, S. & Gintis, H. 'Social capital and community governance', *The Economic Journal*, vol.112, 783, p.419.

4 PERSONAL RESPONSIBILITY

1. See, for example, Glassner, B. (1999) *The Culture of Fear*, Basic Books, New York.

2. See the various essays in Burnside, J. & Baker, N. (eds) (1994) *Relational Justice: Repairing the Breach*, Waterside Press, Winchester.

3. Luke, G. & Lind, B. (2002) 'Reducing juvenile crime: Conferencing verses court', *Crime and Justice Bulletin*, no.69, NSW Bureau of Crime Statistics, Sydney.

5 WORK AND RELATIONSHIPS

1. Cully, M. (2002) 'The cleaner, the waiter, the computer operator: Job change 1986–2001', *Australian Bulletin of Labour*, vol.28, no.3, September.
2. Australian Bureau of Statistics (2002) *Employee Earnings and Trade Union Membership 6310.0*, Canberra.
3. Australian Bureau of Statistics (2000) *Survey of Employment Arrangements and Superannuation 6361.0*, Canberra.
4. Hamilton, C. (2002) 'Overconsumption in Australia: The Rise of the Middle Class Battler', Australia Institute Discussion Paper No. 49, Canberra, p.vii.
5. ibid., p.viii.
6. ibid., p.vii; Hamilton, C. & Mail, E. (2003) 'Downshifting in Australia: A Sea Change in Pursuit of Happiness', Australia Institute Discussion Paper No. 50, Canberra, p.vii.
7. Gittins, R. (2002) 'Relax with Bracks say voters', *The Age*, 4 December 2002.
8. Hamilton & Mail, op. cit., p.17.
9. Hamermesh, D. & Lee, J. (2002) 'Stressed Out on Four Continents: Time Crunch or Yuppie Kvetch?', Preliminary paper, University of Texas, Austin.
10. See speech by ACTU President Sharan Burrow (2003) 'Family Friendly Workplace – the 21st Century Challenge', National Press Club, Canberra, March.
11. *Ex Parte H.V. McKay* (1907) 2.CAR.1.
12. Reported in O'Malley, S. (2003) 'Family friendly victory', *Herald-Sun*, 13 January.

6 CONNECTING WITH YOUNG MEN

1. Australian Bureau of Statistics (2002) *Schools Australia 4221.0*, Canberra, p.11.
2. Rothman, S. (2002) *Longitudinal Surveys of Australian Youth: Achievement in Literacy and Numeracy by Australian 14 year olds 1975-98, Research Report No.29*, ACER, November.
3. See L. Topp et al. (2002) *Australian Drug Trends 2001*, National Drug and Alcohol Research Council, p.120.
4. Australian Bureau of Statistics (1996) *National Crime Statistics 1995 4510.0*, Canberra; (2003) *Recorded Crime Australia 1997–2002 4510.0*, Canberra.
5. Australian Bureau of Statistics (2002) *Suicide 2001*, Canberra.
6. Cully, op. cit.
7. Faludi, S. (1999) *Stiffed*, Chatto & Windus, London, p.530 et seq.
8. House of Representatives Standing Committee on Education and Training (2002) *Boys: Getting it Right*, Canberra.
9. ibid., p.7.
10. ibid., p.135.

11. ibid., p.42.
12. ibid., p.55.
13. Cleary, P. (2002) 'Business failing the skills test', *Australian Financial Review*, 19 August.
14. Data cited by John Buchanan of the Australian Centre for Industrial Relations Research and Training, in *Cleary*, ibid.
15. Quoted in *Cleary*, ibid.
16. This commitment was flagged in Federal Opposition Leader Simon Crean's Budget Reply speech, *Hansard*, 15 May 2003, p.14497. It was first suggested to me by my colleague Christian Zahra, MP.

7 RELATIONAL PARENTING

1. Department of Family and Community Services (1999) *Fitting Fathers Into Families*, Canberra, p.3.
2. ibid., p.vii.
3. ibid., p.14.
4. Australian Bureau of Statistics (2001) *Labour Force Status – Families 6224.0*, Canberra.
5. Smyth, B. & Ferro, A. (2002) 'When the difference is night and day', *Family Matters*, no.63, Spring/Summer, p.56.
6. ibid., p.55.
7. ibid., p.54.
8. *Fitting Fathers Into Families*, op. cit., p.12.
9. Szego, J. (2002) 'High divorce rate not all bad says Chief Justice', *The Age*, 3 September.
10. Weatherburn, D. (2001) 'What causes crime?', *Crime and Justice Bulletin*, NSW Bureau of Crime Statistics and Research, no.54, February, p.4.
11. Turnbull, M. (2002) 'The Tyranny of Proximity', Sydney University Lecture, 17 September.

9 DIGITAL RELATIONSHIPS

1. Schluter & Lee, *The R Option*, op cit, p.37.
2. Friedman, T. (1999) *The Lexus and the Olive Tree*, Farrar Straus & Giroux, New York.

10 HUMANITY AND RELATIONSHIPS

1. Kennedy, L. (1961) *Ten Rillington Place*, Simon & Schuster, New York.
2. See, for example, E. Ullman (2002) 'The post-humans', *Australian Financial Review*, 4 October.
3. See Joy's comments in 'The other Bill', *The Economist Technology Quarterly*, 21 September 2002, p.23.

4. Lewis, C.S. (1944) *The Abolition of Man*, Touchstone, New York, quoted in F. Fukuyama (2002) *Our Posthuman Future*, Farrar, Straus & Giroux, New York, p.7.

5. Fukuyama, op. cit., pp.12-13.

6. ibid.

7. ibid., pp.82, 217-218.

8. ibid., pp.13, 129 et seq.

INDEX

ABOUT THE AUTHOR

Lindsay Tanner is a leading generator of new ideas in Australian politics. He is Shadow Minister for Communications and has held the Federal seat of Melbourne for the ALP since 1993. He was previously Victorian State Secretary of the Federated Clerks Union. Lindsay Tanner has written extensively on political and economic issues, and is the co-author of *The Politics of Pollution*, and author of *The Last Battle* and *Open Australia*, also published by Pluto Press.

In *Open Australia*, Lindsay Tanner argues that the simple question, 'Is Australia to be an open or a closed society?', underpins virtually all major issues in contemporary Australia, and that our actions now will determine whether we go forward in the 21st century as a prosperous, creative and generous nation or decline into a mean and insular backwater.

PRAISE FOR 'OPEN AUSTRALIA'

'Lindsay Tanner's important book challenges us to think about Australia's future in new ways. His sharp analysis, the urgency of his voice and the thoughtfulness of his policy prescriptions will shape the vital debate about the sort of country we should be creating here at the beginning of the 21st century.' – Paul Keating

'Lindsay Tanner's *Open Australia* is a wise, wide ranging, compassionate and thoughtful analysis of the problems facing not only Australia, but the Western social democratic tradition. He has made a major contribution to opening the argument which will go on well into the 21st century. Tanner is already an important thinker. His book deserves close study.' – Barry Jones

THE HAWKE GOVERNMENT – A CRITICAL RETROSPECTIVE

Edited by Susan Ryan and Troy Bramston

Marking the 20th anniversary of the election of the first Hawke Labor Government, *The Hawke Government – A Critical Retrospective* is a collection of essays by a who's who of writers in the fields of politics, academia and the media. It pulls no punches with its insider accounts and its critical outside observations. This publication makes a significant contribution to the written political history of Australia and is set to become the chief record of the people and events of the Hawke period in Australian politics.

Contributors to the book include Craig McGregor, Michael Gordon, Amanda Buckley, Alan Mitchell, Gerard Henderson, Neal Blewett, Graham Freudenberg, Bob Hogg, Tony Moore, Ralph Willis, John Button, Phillip Toyne, Stephen Duckett, Julian Disney, Brian Howe, Di Yerbury, John Kerin, Anne Davies, Warren Snowdon, Pat Dodson, Martin Mowbray, Mary Kalantzis, Bill Kelty, Kim Beazley, Michael Keating, David Bradbury, David Day, Geoff Kitney, Barry Jones, Jim McMorrow, John Warhurst, Jim Chalmers, Susan Ryan and Troy Bramston.

FROM THE SUBURBS

Mark Latham

'People have high expectations about Labor, the party of reform and progressive ideas. No one ever expects the Coalition to do much – they just preside, preen themselves and put the country to sleep.

'The weight is always on Labor to do things. That's why people are keen to know what we stand for. *From the Suburbs* takes up this challenge, from an outer suburban perspective. It uses issues and insights from my electorate of Werriwa, in Sydney's south-west, to advocate new Labor policies.' – Mark Latham

LOCAL HEROES

Kathleen McPhllips

Local Heroes tells the stories of everyday Australians who have been at the front line of a community struggle to rid their local environment of pollution and contamination. Faced with a crisis in their own locality or home, they tell how they were forced to deal with the political reality of fighting for the rights of communities and families at risk.

These stories – full of hope and heroism – tell of how a single person, in deciding to find out why decisions were being made and who was making them, got together with their neighbours to commit themselves to changing what was clearly wrong. In the process, their lives – and the lives of thousands more – were transformed.